A
FOUNDATIONAL BORN,
U.S. AMERICAN

DEDICATION TO:

My Mother, who pushed me to finalize this book whenever I lost the desire to do so. Her constant soft and sobering interrogation; while lying disabled in her bed; "son where you at with your book"? energized my spirit when the breath of motivation had left. She left this realm twelve days after her Eighty-Second birthday. I apologize for being late, but hopefully our second message will be right on time.

"African-Americans built this nation; you built this nation. You know, you are just

starting to get real credit for that. We all built it, but you're such a massive part of it.

Bigger than you were given credit for".

President DONALD J TRUMP

Table of Contents

INTRODUCTION

Growing up in the city called the Big-Easy I realize that a pivotal point in my life began at the youthful age of eleven years old. When I was in the sixth grade I got my first j-o-b as a paperboy. At the age of eleven I joined the Boys Scouts where my brother was elected Scouts Leader, and Mr. Woodie White was our Scouts Master. I owe many expressions of gratitude to the local church I grew up in for sponsoring the growth of my future, and that is to Saint John's Missionary Baptist Church in New Orleans.

Also, at the age of eleven I began my musical journey starting with piano lessons. From there I learned how to play woodwind instruments. I wanted to join the impressive list of musicians from New Orleans that gave birth to Jazz, Zydeco, and even Dixieland. Talents like Wynton Marsalis performing with the National Philharmonic Orchestra, or his brother Bradford Marsalis, who became the Maestros for the Tonight Show Band, hosted by Jay Leno. Or the famous Toussaint Brothers who now lectures in the halls of academia. But most of all, it was my high school, alumni Terrance Blanchard. You may recognize his name from the movies directed by producer Spike Lee. Terrance Blanchard wrote the musical score sheet for all his movies.

But along my journey I experienced musical burn out. So, I channel my endeavor into what I do now. However, I still carry the memories and the universal appreciation that music taught me in my growth.

I begin this manuscript with a speech our Forty-Fifth President spoke the above words to a crowd of youths during a summit in the White House sponsored by Turning Point USA, as reported by Amber Athey, of the Daily Caller. The President amplified a lot more sentiments to the audience during this speech. However, the question is, who exactly are these Black Americans the president is crediting for their massive contribution to the birth of a brand-new nation?

If we look back at this nation's first civil rights organizers beginning in the Eighteen Hundreds, those people were identified as "Colors", as encrypted on the birth certificates of my in-laws, who were born in the Nineteen Sixties in Mississippi. The once-relevant National Association for the Advancement of Colored People (NAACP) founded in 1909 by W.E.B. DuBois and others were named after. So, my ancestors were called people-of-color as early as the Nineteen Hundreds. Later, those people were identified as "Negroes" in the Nineteen Sixties, as encrypted on my Louisiana birth certificate.

However, during the Nineteen Eighties, the Reverend Jessie Jackson introduced the term "African Americans" (AA). He was the face of the once-political activist organization called Rainbow Push Excel, founded in his hometown of Chicago, Illinois.

"Let's Keep Hope Alive" was his gimmick. I remember that era vividly because the Reverend Jackson spoke at the high school, I attended my sophomore year in New Orleans. The phrase African-American was met with sour opposition at the time because it erases our birthright, our planetary history, and our memorial in America. So, we have no language, economy, or culture with Africa.

Africa is not a race of people. Instead, Africa is a large land mass or continent with more than fifty sovereign countries. The citizens there identify themselves by their rich and historical Tribal families. For example, I am Tutsi, from Rwanda, or I am Boka Haram, from Nigeria. This was the tribe who made international buzzfeed when they kidnapped elementary school aged Nigerian girls, then performed jiu- jitsu style surgery upon their genitals. Nonetheless, that title has been used to describe the people the forty-fifth president recognized to this day. Since the corporate and political funds allocated to that organization ended, their slogan has been co-opted by another political activist movement that is sponsored by possibly the same corporate and political donors.

But with the influx of migration into the United States, the term African Americans can no longer be used to identify those people. For example, Elon Musk, the founder of Tesla, Inc, and SpaceX, was born in Pretoria, South Africa. He is now a resident in the United States. He identifies as Afrikaans-American. Certainly, Afrikaans (White South Africans), and African migrants are not the people the President recognized in that speech.

The migrant situation today is buzz-feed throughout the United States, especially under the current Forty-Sixth Administration, with their open border policies. The influx of undocumented migrants coming from the Latin countries of Central American, South America, and the Caribbean-West Indie Islands calling themselves:

Mestizos-Tieno Indians mixed with Europeans,

Mulattos-Latino Afro, mixed with Europeans,

Zambos-Tieno Indians mixed with Africans,

Who are leaving sovereign states with their own governments, elected officials, economy, currency, GDP, language, legal system, education, dialects, diets, and their own culture that they bring with them. Absolutely, these cannot be those the president recognized.

In this book we will ferret out exactly who the President was addressing in his speech, by taking an abbreviated history lesson beginning with the birth of this nation, and the bonds people who burden the landscape for what this land of endless opportunities represent to this date. Here is the legacy of a small population of about twelve percent of the nation; the "Foundational Born, U.S. Americans" descendants.

THE COLONIST FIRST EVER ECONOMY

The Englishmen landed on the American shores in the 1400s. However, there is no historical history of development in this land during that timeframe worth sharing. It was the institution of chattel slavery that developed gradually in the English seaboard colonies. The first slave labor landed INCONUS (Inside the continental U.S.) around 1619. However, there was African slave trading going on around the South Sea's, Central America, and Caribbean Islands long before this period. Since the U.S. Government never colonized any African nations or French, Portuguese, or Spanish territories outside its borders, this volume primarily focuses on the history of INCONUS. Historian Jordan Winthrop records a notice announcing the arrival of slaves to be sold at an auction in Charleston, South Carolina:

"TO BE SOLD on Thursday the third Day of August next, A CARGO of Ninety-Four prime, healthy NEGROES, CONSISTING OF Thirty-nine Men, Fifteen Boys, Twenty-four Women, and Sixteen Girls, just arrived, In the Brigantine Dembia, Francis Bare, Mafter, from Sierra Leon, by DAVID & JOHN DEAS". Charlestown, July 24th, 1769".

To expedite and increase the numbers for free slave labor, legislators began ratifying laws such as the "one-drop rule". This rule had nothing to do with science or human biology, requiring twenty-three selected chromosomes from each parent to form a zygote. It stated, "Children born of a mother in a state of slavery, follow the condition of their mother; they are consequently slaves, and belong to the master of their mother" (Louisiana Article 183). (So here, once again, statues were passed to exonerate the planters of the colonial era from their promiscuities. As a show of dominance, the planter would often accost the enslaved woman in the quarters where she rested. In front of her younger children, and in front of the enslaved man alongside them. This act gave birth to a new expression in the English lexicon, Motherf*****. When the negro child saw the planter, or his brother, or his uncle, or his son in the fields, they would address them as the MF).

Also, this statue piggy-back from a previous rule called the "blood quantum law" which stated any indigenous individual who was less than one-half Indian, was not Indian, and could not claim any rights to their land. The one-drop rule increased the number of negro slaves for free labor. Whereas the quantum rule was used to decrease the number of Indians, clearing for white expansionism and erasing native identities. The quantum law will be discussed in a later chapter. For now, I want to highlight how Article 183 rescued the families of whites from any obligation of airing property, insurance, monetary benefits, freedom, or any other type of estate, to their biracial enslaved children.

For example, President Thomas Jefferson was the father to six children born of a enslave woman named Sally Hemings. Sally was a biracial child, born of a biracial slave woman name Elizabet Betty. Sally's father was a white man whose name was never listed. From 1773-1835, Sally was the President's housemaid, seamstress, and nursemaid. Eventually, the President freed two of their children but left the remaining four in slavery.

Martha Jefferson, the oldest daughter of the President and his former wife, tried to deny the paternity of her father to any of Sallies children. Due to the advancements in medicine, a DNA test was conducted on two male Aire's of the President in 1998, and it was determined that the President was indeed the father of all six of Sally children. Later, it was discovered that the President   freed the remaining four adult children in his Will after he died. But only his children. He did not free any family members his adult children berth.

I randomly looked up the definition of child support laws. Here is what I came up with:

The legal definition of child support (according to Legal Dictionary) is funds ordered by the court for one parent to pay the other to assist in the cost of raising their shared children. Support is, most often, determined by a standardized income table and factors in the number of children, incomes of both parents and the custody arrangement.

I could not find a statute of limitations. So, let's imagine   that each State assists the descendants of these children, then compensates them in any form of revenue for the lack of support, funds, torture, and slavery   they endured.

Cotton became king. Historian Dan Allosso recorded the following essay regarding cotton. "In the years before the civil war, American planters in the Sough continued to grow Chesapeake tobacco and Carolina rice as they had in the colonial era. Cotton, however, emerged as the antebellum south's major commercial crop, eclipsing tobacco, rice, and sugar in economic importance. By 1860, the region produced two-thirds of the world's cotton. As a commodity, cotton also had the advantage of being easily stored and transported. Demand in the industrial textile mills of Great Britain and New England seemed inexhaustible. Southern cotton, picked and processed by American slaves, upheld the wealth and power of the planter elite. At the same time, it fueled the nineteenth-century industrial revolution in both colonial American and Britain.

Almost no cotton was grown in the colonies in 1790 when the first Census was conducted (that census only counted white males). Following the War of 1812, cotton became the key cash crop of the southern economy and the most important colonial commodity. By 1850, one point eight million of the three-point two million slaves in the country's fifteen slave states produced cotton and by 1860, slave labor produced over two billion pounds of cotton annually. The colonist cotton made up two-thirds of the global supply, and production continued to increase. By the time of the civil war, South Carolina politician James Hammond confidently proclaimed that the North could never threaten the South because 'cotton is king'.

The crop grown in the South was a hybrid known as Petit Gulf cotton that grew extremely well in the Mississippi River Valley and other states like Texas. Whenever new slave states entered the Union, white slaveholders sent armies of slaves to clear land to grow the lucrative crop. This force migration from the upper southern states to the deep south, lower on the Mississippi, to grow cotton. The enslaved people forced to build James Hammonds cotton kingdom and their labor started by clearing the land. Thomas Jefferson's agrarian vision of white yeoman farmers settling the West by single-handedly carving out small independent farms ironically proved quite different in the South. Old-growth Forest and cypress swamps were cleared by slaves and readied for plowing and planting. To ambitious white planters, the new land available for cotton production seemed almost limitless. Many planters leapfrogged from one area to the next, abandoning their fields every ten to fifteen years when the soil became exhausted. Slaves composed the vanguard of this American expansion to the West".

Cotton became so popular worldwide, especially in Colonial America and Britain, American planters scrambled to invest more in cotton, and less in tobacco in the Chesapeake, rice in the Carolina's, and sugar in Louisiana. To this day, read the label on the apparel you wear, the sheets on your beds, well you get the details.

The demand for textile mills in Britain caused inexhaustible business for cotton field landowners, who drafted consent decrees to work their slaves from sun-up to sun-down in the name of production. Dan Allosso continues to write, "Following the War of 1812, cotton became the key cash crop of the southern economy. By 1850, one point eight million of the three-point-two million slaves in the   country's fifteen slave states produced cotton. And by 1860, fortunately for us, slave labor produced over two billion pounds of cotton annually. Colonial America cotton made up two-thirds of the global supply. Petit Gulf cotton grew in the Mississippi Valley and Texas area. White slaveholders sent armies of slaves to clear land to grow lucrative crop. Old-growth forests and cypress swamps were cleared by Slaves and readied for plowing and planting. Many slaveowners leap frogged from one area to the next, abandoning their fields every ten to fifteen years when the soil became exhausted. Slaves composed the vanguard of this American expansion to the West".

As the greed for cotton forges it's way further and further west. The need to connect the sough equal to that of the north. The sough invested heavily in free slave labor to further their ideas. The Appalachian Mountains, Arkansas, Missouri, and Texas demonstrated the large growth of their economy at the hands of railroads   and the free labor obtained from enslaved men, women, and children.

Southern railroad companies bought slaves and used them to construct their line. Thousands of negros an built their lines in the 1850's. By the 1860's, southern territories were the third leading railroad region in the world. Trailing the North   and Britain.

The economy in Colonial America was flourishing. It created a desire for industrialization, such as ironworkers. Historian Charles Dew wrote "Though what is called the Iron District, on the Cumberland and Tennessee Rivers, there are from eight to ten thousand enslaved people at the iron works... assembled in large numbers, working in the various labors of making charcoal, digging ore, and tending the furnaces, in gangs mostly by themselves, with a few whites for general overseers. This enumeration marked an expansion of the iron industry   in this district. Between 1852 and 1856, no less than twelve new blast furnaces were constructed, five older furnaces were rebuilt and returned to production, and two new forges were erected along the Cumberland and Tennessee rivers; these installations probably raised the number of slave ironworkers in the area to approximately three thousand men. However, whites outnumbered blacks in each county comprising the iron district. The introduction of even greater numbers of industrial slaves, and the relative isolation of many of the ironworks could easily lead to heightened fears of slave uprisings in a year of political turmoil and uncertainty and of widespread and well-publicized insurrectionary rumors".

BILL OF SALE FOR SOUTH CAROLINA SLAVES,

"This February 22, 1827, bill describes the sale of a dozen South Carolina slaves-Dolly, Jacke, Jemmy, Grace, Dinah, Liddy, John and infant, Paul, Hagar, Jack and Jane, from the estate of Arnoldus Vanderhorst, deceased; to Edward Frost for Three Thousand and Twenty Dollars."

Edward Frost was the President of the Blue Ridge Railroad in South Carolina.

Historian William Thomas wrote, "Slaveholding expanded in the Wiregrass and in the Appalachian Mountains, and commercial agriculture developed in the wake of the railroads. The fastest-growing regions of the South, especially along the western border of Texas, Arkansas, and Missouri, demonstrated just how compatible slavery was with the southern railroad growth. The railroads began purchasing enslaved men away from their enslavers between the ages of Sixteen to Thirty-five, beginning in 1841. They recorded these events in balance sheets and company account books. The companies used Bills of Sales, and Contracts where they included insurance clauses because, after all, the companies were liable to the enslavers for the lost, or injury their slave incurred". The labor that the slave produced was paid in revenues to the slaveholder, or their estate. But never to the slave. "All that a slave possesses belongs to his master; he possesses nothing of his own, except his peculium (personal property as might be held by a slave) - that is to say, the sum of money or movable estate which his master chooses he should possess" (Louisiana Article 175).

Legislators in Colonial America implemented crushing statues, with coils of lethal enforcement mechanisms, that crippled every imaginable self-sufficiency (or pull yourself up by your bootstraps) of the slave labor force. But, in turn, it enriched the institution of slavery religiously.

In a lecture to his stockholders, the president of the Mississippi Central Railroad stated, "I am led to the irresistible conclusion, that in ease of management, in the economy of maintenance, in the certainty of execution of work & amount of labor performed & in the absence of disturbance of riotous outbreaks, the slave is, preferable to fee labor, and far better adapted to the construction of railways in the south."

SOUTH-CAROLINA.

Whereas the Honourable Court of Equity, by their Decree made at Charleston during _January_ sitting, eighteen hundred and twenty-_seven_

did direct that certain Negroes, belonging to _the Estate of Highland Vanderhurst deceased_

should be sold by the Master of the said Court, on terms in said Decree specified, all of which will more particularly appear on reference to the Registry of the Court: And whereas, at a sale of the said Negroes before me, as Master in Equity, at Charleston, on the _twenty fourth_ day of _February_ eighteen hundred and twenty-_seven_ the following Negro Slaves named _Dolly, Lucka, Sammy, Mary, Nancy, Little John and an Infant, Paul, Peggy, Bob and Sam_

purchased by _Edward Frost_ for the sum of _Three thousand and twenty Dollars_

Now Therefore, I MATHEW IRVINE KEITH, as Master of the said Court by virtue of the authority in me vested, under the Decree above-mentioned, and also for and in consideration of the said sum of _Three thousand and twenty Dollars_

by the said _Edward Frost_ paid,
Do Hereby bargain and sell unto to the said _Edward Frost_ the above _recited_ Negro, To Have and to Hold the said _recited_ Negro, together with the further issue of the Females

to the only proper use of the said _Edward Frost_ his Heirs, Executors, Administrators and Assigns.

In Witness whereof, I have hereunto set my Hand and Seal, this _twenty fourth_ day of _February_ in the year of our Lord one thousand eight hundred and twenty _seven_ and of the American Republic the _fifty first_

THE REVOLUTIONARY WAR

The very first war on America's soil was the Revolutionary War of 1775. It involved the British Soldiers or the Redcoats stationed as overseers and enforcers of the Queen of England agenda. Her agenda was to enrich and empower the homeland at the sacrifice of the Newfoundland, native indigenous, and human slaves, consisting of colonial America with passive aggressive laws, taxation, religious subjugation, and many other oppressive laws from the chair of the Throne.

The imposition of the "Stamp Act" forged the colonist's rebellion away from the throne. The Stamp Act places the British stamp of ownership onto all bills of note's, receipts, deeds, contracts, and legal papers. As well as required the colonist to affix revenues, namely stamps on all official document that were to be delivered across the pond, to the Queen for her ownership. Remnants of the Stamp Act exist in the United States today. Property owners are never really property owners, in that unpaid property taxes could cause the State to confiscate said property, even if the deed of said sis that the tax from the said property is needed to operate the services rendered to everyone within its jurisdiction.

It is written in history that the firing of a crowd of unarmed civilians outside of a tavern in Massachusetts, known as the "Boston Massacre," was the act that sparked the revolt known as the Revolutionary War. The soldiers who fired the shots reported they "feared for their lives".

One civilian who was fired upon, Michael Johnson, or "Crispus Attucks", was the son of a slave father and a native aboriginal mother who escaped bondage as a run-away. For his reward, Deacon William Brown wrote, "Ten pounds reward for the return of a negro fellow, about twenty-seven years of, named Crispus, six feet, two inches high, short curled hair". Crispus was memorialized as one of the first attackers who rushed the soldiers to defend the slain. A Boston lawyer, John Adams, disapproved of the mob Crispus led against the red coats. He declared that Crispus had led a "motley rabble saucy boys, negroes".

John Hancock, a merchant, asked, "Who taught the British soldier that he might be defeated? Who dared look into his eyes? I place, the, therefore, this Crispus Attucks in the foremost rank of the men that dared".

John Adams copied in his diaries anonymous letters written to the Governor of Massachusetts, Thomas Hutchinson in 1773 that read "you ought to hear from us in horror. You are chargeable before God and Man, with our blood. You acted coolly, deliberately, with all that premeditated malice, not against us, but the people in general. You will hear further from us hereafter". And it was signed as "Crispus Attucks".

Later it was the famous words of Patrick Henry who called "slavery of negroes" repugnant to humanity", and who patriotic Americans today repeat these words, "give me liberty or give me death" But Patrick Henry was viewed with a side eye; because he was an owner of slaves when he wrote those words.

It was a pamphlet written by a Quaker, Anthony Benezette in 1766 "A caution and a Warning to Great Britain and Her Colonies to the treatment of thousands and tens of thousands of our fellow men, who...are at this very time kept in the most deplorable state of slavery. Nonetheless, in April of 1783 the Revolutionary War officially ended. And a peace treaty was signed in Paris five months later. But mighty King George defied the reality that   a colony of rag-tag militia men, and enslaved Black people defeated the British. The gave the defeat largely in part to the colony's superior alleys of Franc and Spain, as they too fought sided by the side against the Crown.

During the celebration back in colonial America at one of the militaries review a French Officer name Jean Baptiste Antoine de Verger became so impressed by the First Rhode Island Regiment that he made a watercolor sketch of the regiment. Baron von Closen of the Continental Army wrote, "the regiment is the most neatly dressed, the best under arms, and the most precise in its maneuvers". They were referring to a regiment with three-quarters of foot soldiers being negroes of slave descent. Post-war, the question arose what colonial America will do with its human slave-like livestock sprinkled amongst the free, the proud, and the brave? So, the continental congress reconvened in Philadelphia, where members of the original congress were absent. However, many representing the Northern territories were bent on abolishing the powers of the south held, and the laws that held slavery entrenched. But the southern representatives were not listening to that, as the South threatened, they would succeed. It was John Ruthledge of South Carolina who posed, "Is the true question at present is whether the southern state shall or shall not be parties to the union" Rutherledge then espoused that "religion and humanity have nothing to do with the question. Interest alone is the governing principle with nations".

The northern representatives declared that the negroes forced into free labor as slaves be left out of southern representation because they systematically could never vote and were not even citizens. However, they were infantrymen in the recent victory over King George. So, the "Three-Fifth Compromise" was raised. It required that southern states would receive one vote for every three-slave man and woman in the South. This clause enabled the South to gain more congressional seats and votes in the Electoral College. The south would either rule; or succeed from the union.

Along with the south dominance, their political representatives invoked that most heinous laws against humankind imaginable. They legally created an entire system of superiority of the white race of people over another, regardless of their political views or region in which they resided. That point of view also established the enforcement mechanism of policing that delivered swift and severe judgement against the race of people their laws were written to subjugate. The "Louisiana Purchase" guaranteed the future of the United States of America to be a permanent colony of British Settlers, aboriginal natives, black bondsmen, and bondswomen. The defeat of Napolean caused the French to sell most of their territories in America for a busted rate of four cents per acre. DeWitt Talmadge, who was a nineteenth-century cleric wrote "all of Indian territory, all of Kansas and Nebraska, Iowa and Wyoming, Montana and the Dakota's, and most of Colorado and Minnesota, and Washington and Oregon states came to us as the indirect work of a despised negro".

The war of 1812 also bore the phrase "uncle Sam". A government inspector inspected military cargo before they were shipped to sea. Samuel "Uncle Sam" Wilson, the leader nicknamed him. The U.S. Navy seaman core serving on warships and supply ships in the war of 1812 was nearly one-sixth negro slaves. Captain Oliver Hazard Perry complained about being sent only enslaved Black people's seaman and boys for nine of the navy's newest ships. His complaint inspired Commodore Isaac Chauncy to reply "they are not surpassed by any of the seaman   we have in the fleet, and I have yet to learn that the color of a man's skin or the cut and trimmings of the coat can affect a man's qualification or usefulness. I have nearly fifty blacks on board this a ship and many of them are among my best men". Of   enslaved Black people serving on supply, or privateers ships as they were called at that time, Nathaniel Shaler, Commander of the ship name "Governor Thompkins wrote in January 1812 the following statement:

"Her first broadside kills two men and wounded others...

The other name of one of my poor fellows was a black man name John Johnson, a

Twenty-four-pound shot struck him in the hip and took away all the lower part of his

Body: in this state the poor brave fellow lay on the deck, exclaimed to his shipmate

Fire away, boys. The other was a black man   by name of John Davis, and was struck.

In much the same way, several times requested to be thrown overboard, saying.

He was only in the way of others".

Part 3

After the Revolutionary War, enslaved Black people were typically banned from military service. Congress passed laws restricting militia service to abled-bodied white male citizens in 1793. Most states enacted laws that put in plain view that backs, bondmen, or freemen cannot be helpful. However, Louisiana had a special clause written into its law on service even though Louisiana was a pro-slavery territory.

Gail Buckley details in her book "American Patriots" how the free black militia in New Orleans in 1803 was called to service. She also highlights a letter written by Governor William Claiborne to President James Madison saying, "that New Orleans black militia was esteemed a very serviceable corps, not to re-commission them would disgust them, and might be productive of future mischief."

Louisiana's laws required all militia officers to be "white men." But the New Orleans black militia had three black officers. They were Joseph Savary, Vincent Populus, and Isidore Honore. I wager if Commanding General Russell L Honore, of the Hurricane Katrina Disaster Task Force in New Orleans, under President George W Bush in 2005, has any connections. In January 2021, the U. S. Congress nominated General Honore to lead the "Capital Riots" in Washington, D.C.

The question arose again when the Assistant Paymaster of the Seventh Military District in the region rejected the idea of paying the black soldiers even as free men and patriotic soldiers. However, Andrew Jackson quashed that idea when he wrote this letter on September 21, 1814, saying:

"Through a mistaken policy, you have previously been deprived of participation in the glorious struggle for national rights in which our country is engaged. This no longer shall exist. As sons

Of freedom, you are called upon to defend our most inestimable blessing. To every noble-hearted generous freeman of color, volunteering to serve during the present contest with Great Britain...there will be paid the same bounty in money and lands now received by white.

25

Soldiers of the United States, viz, one hundred and twenty-four dollars in money   and one Hundred and sixty acres of land".

The New Orleans black militia and all the other black soldiers storm forward into battle but as segregated infantrymen. As the war of 1812 ended, the British armadas retreated from the bayous in the Chalmette Plains, the Rodriguez Canal. President John Adams acknowledged that New Orleans was the worst British military defeat since the Revolution. That the new country for fighting for a country, not just thirteen colonies. Only a few black soldiers received pensions after the war of 1812. However, none of the black soldiers received any portion of the one hundred sixty acres of land General Andrew Jackson promised them. To this date, that promise is still owed. Suppose the humanity inside you leads you to phantom that life in colonial American forged her in the direction of freeing her chain and tethered, free human labor. In that case, you are in for more disappointments. The Southern States tightened the free movement of the enslaved people with laws just short of regulating the blinking of their eyes. Edwin C Holland, of Charleston, South Carolina, 1822 wrote, "Let it never be forgotten, that our Negroes are freely the Jacobins of the country."

After the Revolutionary War, President George Washington proposed the idea of an official Military Academy. Around 1802, West Point was founder above the Hudson River in Jew York. General Robert E Lee, Stonewall Jackson, and Ulysses S Grant were all among the first graduates. Soon after, the Naval Academy was established around 1845 in Annapolis Maryland. It was congressionally established that Negro service members would not be trained as cadets or plebes to become officers.

James W Smith was the first Negro to qualify for West Point in 1870, and John H Conyers was the first Negro to get admitted into Annapolis in 1872. But soon after his admission, James Smith received one court inquiry, and two court martials. He was forced to turn in his resignation via threats from faculty and sabotage from fellow classmates.

John Conyers admission was unscrupulously taken away at Annapolis in 1873 for similar reasons. It was Henry O Flipper, who was born in rural Georgia that became the first Negro graduate from West Point. William Nell in his book "Colored Patriots of the American Revolution" described Flippers graduation:

"When Mr. Flipper, the colored cadet, stepped forward and received the rewards of four years of hard work and unflinching courage as any young man can be called upon to go through, the crowd gave him a round of applause. It was General Sherman himself who presented Henry Flipper with his diploma. And the one who announced that 'I shall certainly shake his flipper when he says goodbye'. West Point classes of 1887 through 1891 began to target Negro soldiers from the Nineth and Tenth Calvary; heroes from the Indian American Wars, to become cadets".

The highly prestige Harvard University was founded in 1636 in Cambridge Massachusetts. Then after, Yale University in New Haven Connecticut, was founded. Their doors of admission were closed to Negros from ever being admitted.

What is known today as Historically Black Colleges & Universities (HBCU's) were formed by post-slave era Negros as far back as 1867 when Howard (The Power) University was built in Washington D.C. They have educated America's best and brightest citizens ever. Then in the same year, the Black Church founded Morehouse (The House) College for males only to attend.

It was not until The Second Morrill Act of 1890 was passed that required all southern states to establish sister universities for Negroes to attend since white universities were segregated and had no intentions of ever admitting them on their campuses. In 1904 Mary McLoud Bethune, the founder of the once pertinent club, League of Negro Women, also established a college for Young Negro Women to attend. Then in 1925 Xavier University in New Orleans, the nation's only predominate black catholic university was founded. There are far too many more HBCU's with stellar achievements for me to list. However, I do recognize them all and am proud of their existence.

THE STARS & STRIPES
VS
THE STARS & BARS

These were two flags that represented two separated countries during the colonial period. The Stars and Stripes served as a sign for the end of the chattel bondage of all negro enslaved people. While the Stars and Bars symbolized life, slavery, then death to all negroes in early America. The only taste of humanity came when the slave's breath their last breath, it was told. William Wells Brown, a formerly enslaved person describes this dilemma in his book "The Black Man", a story his mother told him of the five-year-old child of the Mistress she worked for in Kentucky. She said "whenever William (the five-year-old) had become impudent, petulant, peevish and cruel. Sitting at the tea table, he would often desire to make his entire meal out of the sweetmeats, sugar bowl, or cake, and when mistress would not allow him to have them, he would throw anything within reach at her in a fit of anger. Spoons, knives, forks, and dishes would be hurled at her head". At the youngest of age, their children were taught to exercise tyranny on slaves, however, whenever, and wherever. Often, the slaves were given the names of the families they labored for. J.D. Thomas posted a blog in 2011 defining slavery and slaves in my home state of Louisiana:

DEFINITIONS OF SLAVES, &c.

- ART. 35. A slave is one who is in the power of a master to whom he belongs. The master may sell him, dispose of his person, his industry, and his labor; he can do nothing, possess nothing, nor acquire anything, but what must belong to his master.
- ART. 38. Freemen are those who have preserved their natural liberty – that is to say, who have the right of doing whatever is not forbidden by law.
- ART. 95. Slaves are incapable of contracting marriage together; the celebration of such marriages is forbidden, and the marriage is void.

29

- ART. 172. The rules prescribing the police and conduct to be observed with respect to slaves in this State, and the punishment of their crimes and offences, are fixed by special laws of the Legislature.
- ART. 174. the slave is incapable of making any kind of contract, except those which relate to his own emancipation.
- ART. 175. All that a slave possesses belongs to his master; he possesses nothing of his own, except his peculium (personal property as might be held by a slave) - that is to say, the sum of money or movable estate which his master chooses he should possess.
- ART. 176. They can transmit nothing by succession (debt passed on by death of the slave) or otherwise.
- ART. 177. The slave is incapable of exercising any public office or private trust; he cannot be tutor, curator, executor, nor attorney; he cannot be a witness in either civil or criminal matters. He cannot be a party in any civil action, either as plaintiff or defendant, except when he has to claim or prove his freedom.
- ART. 178. When slaves are prosecuted for offences, they have committed, notice must be given to their masters.
- ART. 179. Master's are bound by the acts of their slaves done by their command; but in case they should not have authorized or instructed them, they shall be answerable only for so much as they have benefited (jusqu'a concurrence de ce qui aura tourne a leur profit [up to a limit of what have worked out for them] [by the transaction.
- ART. 180. The master shall be answerable for all the damages occasioned by an offence or quasi offence committed by his slave, independent of the punishment inflicted on the slave.
- ART. 181. The master may discharge himself from such responsibility by abandoning his slave to the person injured; in which case, such person shall sell such slave at public auction, in the usual form, to obtain payment of the damages and costs, and the balance, if any, shall be returned to the master.

- ART. 182. Slaves cannot marry without the consent of their masters, and their marriages do not produce any of the civil effects which result from such contract.
- ART. 183. Children born of a mother then in a state of slavery, whether married or not, follow the condition of their mother; they are consequently slaves, and belong to the master of their mother.
- ART. 184. A master may manumit (liberate) his slave either by an act inter vivos, (a gift or to give away) or by a disposition made in prospect of death, provided such emancipation be made with the forms and under the conditions prescribed by law.
- ART. 185. No one can emancipate his slave unless the slave has attained the age of thirty years and has behaved well at least for four years preceding his emancipation.
- ART. 186. The slave who has saved the life of his master, his master's wife, or one of his children, may be emancipated at any age.
- ART. 187. The master who wishes to emancipate his slave is bound to make a declaration of his intentions to the judge of the parish (counties) where he resides; the judge must order notice of it to be published during forty days and if, at the expiration of this delay, no opposition be made, he shall authorize the master to pass the act of emancipation.
- ART. 188. The act of emancipation imports an obligation, on the part of the person granting it, to provide for the subsistence of the slave emancipated, if he should be unable to support himself.
- ART. 189. An emancipation is irrevocable on the part of the master or his heirs.
- ART. 190. Any enfranchisement made in fraud of creditors, or of the portion reserved by law to forced heirs, is null and void; if the slave manumitted was specially mortgaged; but in this case the enfranchisement shall take effect, provided the slave, or any one on his behalf, shall pay the debt for which the mortgage was given.
- ART. 191. No master of slaves shall be compelled to enfranchise any slave, except in cases where the enfranchisement shall be made for services rendered to the

31

State, and on the state paying to the master the appraised value of the manumitted slave.

- ART. 192. In like manner, no master shall be compelled to sell his slave, but in one of two cases to wit: first, when, being only co-proprietor of the slave, his co-proprietor demands the sale, in order to make partition of the property; the second, when the master shall be convicted of cruel treatment of his slave, and the judge shall deem proper to pronounce, besides the penalty established for such cases, that the slave shall be sold at public auction, in order to place him out of reach of the power which his master has abused.

- ART. 193. The slave who has acquired the right of being free at a future time, is from that time capable of receiving, by testament or donation. Property given or devised to him must be preserved for him, in order to be delivered to him in kind when his emancipation shall take place.

- ART. 196. The child born of a woman after she has acquired the right of being free at a future time, follows the condition of its mother, and becomes free at the time fixed for her enfranchisement, even if the mother should die before that time.

- ART. 221. The acknowledgment of an illegitimate child shall be made by a declaration executed before a notary public, in presence of two witnesses, whenever it shall not have been made in the registering of the birth or baptism of such child. No other proof of acknowledgment shall be admitted in favor of children of color.

- ART. 226. Free illegitimate children of color may also be allowed to prove their descent from a father of color only.

- ART. 230. Illegitimate children of every description may make proof of their natural maternal descent, provided the mother be not a married woman.

- ART. 322. The following persons cannot be tutors, to wit: Slaves.

- ART. 492. The children of slaves and the young of animals belong to the proprietor of the mother of them, by right of accession.

- ART. 631. He who has the use of one or more slaves or animals has the right to enjoy their service for his wants and those of his family.
- ART. 945. All free persons, even minors, lunatics, persons of insane mind, and the like, may transmit their estates ab intestato, and inherit from others.
- Slaves alone are incapable of either.
- ART. 1361. Where slaves have been given the donee is not permitted to collate them in kind; he is bound to collate for them by taking less, according to the value of the slaves at the time of the donation.
- ART. 1362. Therefore, the donation of slaves contains an absolute transfer of the rights of the donor to the donee, in the slaves thus given. They are at the risk of the donee, who is bound to support their loss or deterioration, at the same time that he profits by the children born of them; and if the donee dispose, in good faith, of all or any of the slaves, the action of revendication for recovering the slaves, on the part of his co-heirs, for the collation due to them, will not be against those who are purchasers or holders of the slaves.
- ART. 1462. Slaves cannot dispose of, or receive by donation inter vivos or mortis causa, unless they have been previously and expressly enfranchised conformably to law, or unless they are expressly enfranchised by the act itself by which the donation is made to them.

All southern states adopted similar legislation in their jurisdictions to prevent negro enslaved people in a restricted state from fleeing to a state with lesser restrictions. These Articles became the law of the land in the South.

Great Britain began abolishing slave trading in late 1833 and emancipating enslaved people in all the West Indies (Caribbean) and Latin territories. However, that was not the case within the borders of America, or today the United States. Slavery and the status of slavery was foreseen as a never-ending free labor class for all white citizens who immigrated to her shores. The words Life, Liberty, and the Pursuit was changed from its original slogan of Life, Liberty, and Property. Property was brightly defined as negro slavery. It is abundantly clear that most white families that immigrated to colonial America were not slave owners. They were too poor in their homeland and America to afford or maintain such an institution. However, the laws were blunt. Slavery was an option for all whites if ever they could afford it.

Abolition groups began to form in the northern states. The Quakers coincided with many white religious groups who believed that the wholesale lynching, burning, or amputation of negro slaves unchecked was a violation of the God they believed in. President Abraham Lincoln told the story of a riverboat ride he once took in 1841; "You and I had together a tedious low water trip on a steamboat from Louisville to St Louis. You may remember as well that from Louisville to the mouth of the Ohio there were on board ten to a dozen slaves' shackle together with irons. That sigh was a continued torment to me, and I see something like it every time in Ohio and border states". The reader can digest that slavery was not just a southern ideology.

However, the southern colonists were the staunchest believers and enforcers of free labor in their territories. By 1861 the south consisted of Alabama, Arkansas, Florida, Georgia, Louisiana, Mississippi, Carolina's, Tennessee, Texas, and Virginia. Missouri soon followed and became a pro-slavery state. The confederate states forged an oath that rather than compromise on the issue of slavery, they would prefer to destroy the Union. Months after the election of the Sixteenth President, Abraham Lincoln in 1860, South Carolina declared itself an independent commonwealth because the President-elect once called the Union a "house divided cannot be permanently half slaves and half free". The President later stated that "the issue is union, not slavery". You, the audience decide Lincoln's stance on this topic.

According to E.B. Long in his book "The Civil War Day by Day," he reported that there was an estimate of 8,099,674 white colonists in the south. And 3,950,511 negro slaves in the south just before the civil war. The white colonists in the north estimated to be 18,901,917. And that northern states had industries and the first military telegraph system. Their monetary system countered the souths cotton mastery. The wealthy white slave owners in the south maintained such a wealthy monopoly over their poor white counterparts that jobs for poor white southerners was mainly; slave drivers or overseers, slave auctioneers, slave constables on patrol (cops) who were readily train and armed to captive, return runaways and to squash any threats of slave uprisings, and to inflect unimaginable amount of great bodily harm without impunity.

W.J. Cash, in his book "The Mid of the South," described poor whites as "if his real interest ran the other way about, he did nevertheless have that to me, the dear treasure of his superiority as a shite man, which was preferred on him by slavery, and so was determined to keep the negro man in chains. Color alone is here the badge of distinction, the true mark of aristocracy, and all white are equal despite the variety of occupation". Professor Thomas R Dew, in his book "Race and history: Selected Essays" concurred. Negroes in the north were considered freed negroes under the law duly based on their free status. However, they were harassed, captured, and returned to southern states for bounties. They were returned to plantation owners on trump-up violations in the north.

So poor white northerners created their monetary system of kidnapping free negro-men bodies, then selling them to southerner plantation owners.

When the war began between the colonies, Congressman implemented escape clauses for whites to be exempt from fighting. For example, the "Conscription Act of 1863" was enacted. This provision allowed enslavers with twenty or more enslaved people to be exempt from war. Or those who could pay three hundred dollars could also be exempt from fighting. It also permitted mega families like the banking magnates J. P. Morgan, Andrew Carnegie, and Admiral Jean P Strouse, who wrote: "By the 1850s cotton accounted for more than half of all-U.S. exports. We are pleased to hear that the only ship that could render the superior British navy useless was the American vessel Cotton". These magnates could pay the fees of Irish immigrants, thereby isolating them from the draft. Many mega families believed that the Irishman should not have to fight in the war to free slaves, who in return would take away their jobs. That mentality fueled the flames in New York into wanton attacks, looting the homes, killings, then burning many of the bodies of the freed negroes in the streets. The victims who survived the riot fled into the nearby catholic church in Manhattan. John Templeton Strong, a lawyer and a diarist, wrote, "the negroes are the most peaceable sober and inoffensive of our poor. I am sorry that England is right about the lower class of Irish. They are brutal, base, cruel, cowards, and as bold as a base. But how can one deal with women who assemble around a lamppost to which a negro hangs and cut off certain parts of his body to keep as a souvenir".

Southern plantation owners financed bounty hunters. In the south. property loss (run away or freed slaves) became intolerable. The penalty for many captured slaves was amputations. On some plantations, runaways had their arm amputated from the shoulder down to the middle finger. Some had a foot amputated from the ankle down. Pregnant negro women had their belly sliced open while standing, then the head of the fetus would be crushed in the ground.

Quakers in the South and the North ramped up their part in assisting slaves to freedom into Canada. First known as the "business of Egypt" the second promise land, and finally, the underground railroad. In 1872 William Still, a station master in Snow Hill, New Jersey, one of the busiest railways in the East, and the son of slaves in the south, had his notes published in a book titled "The Underground Railroad". William, who was the owner of his own locomotor, "The Liberty Line" advertise:

"The improved and splendid locomotives fitted in the best style of accommodation.

for passengers will run their regular trips between the borders of Patriarchal Dominion and

Libertyville, Upper Canada irrespective of color".

In his diaries, William kept notes of the runaways who passed through his station so that family or friends could reunite. The slaves were hidden in compartments underneath the floors of the railway, covered by designs and hidden panels.

But Harriet Tubman is known for her heroics in the underground railroad era. She was called "The Female Moses". Her motive was to lead as many runaway slaves to freedom as she could humanly free. Harriet was born into slavery in 1820 on a plantation in Maryland, another non southern state. Harriet was beaten so badly by her slave mistress that she was permanently scarred on her face and neck. Saying "if you do not stop whipping that child, I will leave your house and never come back" said the sister of the child abuser. According to Sarah Bradford, a white abolitionist who authored the book "Scenes in the Life of Harriet Tubman".

Even with posters offering forty thousand dollars in rewards for her capture, dead or alive, Harriet continued her mission to guide runaway slaves to their freedom. On her plantation, Harriet had her skull split open by one of her overseers with a weight scale because she refused to help tie up a young slave boy to get beat with a whip. Harriet experienced lifelong seizures from that one blow. The plantation owner tried to sell her, but no one purchased her. Harriet succeeded in escaping when her plantation owner died. During that time, she began helping her father and mother, who were on two different plantations, run using the underground railroad. Harriet then led her ten brothers and sisters to their freedom. Once on the railways, messages were codified in slave hymns. For example, "hail oh hail ye happy spirits" meant safety. Buth when "go down Moses" was   sung, that meant danger was nearing. They would pacify infant children with opium to keep them quiet while hidden on freedom trains. The runaways who became abhorrent or disrespectful during the journey, Harriet met them with her shot gun to continue or get shot to death.

Harriet Tubman died in 1913. One of her most torching statements ridiculing Harriet Beecher Stowe, a poet who tried to commercialize slavery for a profit with her stage play "Uncle Toms Cabin", she said of the play, "I aint got no heart to go and see the suffering of my people played on de stage. I've heard the story read to me, and Miss Stowe's pen hasn't begun to paint what slavery is. I've seen de real ting, and I don't want to see it on no stage or in no later". Harriet Tubman is forever my hero.

During the war between the States, one Major General John C Fremont, who was the Commander of the Western Department, issued a proclamation that all slaves who took up arms for the Union would be free. However, that proclamation infuriated President Lincoln extensively that he fired that general.

It was the Kansas Volunteers, the first all slave fighting unit in 1862 to actually engage in combat, as they repelled a superior confederate guerrilla force near Butler Missouri, the Leavenworth Conservative newspaper wrote, "the men fought like tigers, every one of them".   In his book "The Sable Arm" in 1987, Dudley Cornish wrote in his book "these are the boys to clean out bushwhackers. The Kansas Volunteers had victories against the Native American soldiers who fought with the Confederates, such as in Island Mound Missouri, and other Indian territories such as Honey Springs. The native American soldiers, on the side of the confederates ere already free men, and women who were compensated hundreds of thousands of acres land that was protected Federal Entities then, as well as to this very day. So, their volunteerism to defend the institution of chattel negro slavery was done so without hesitation. Not all Indian Tribes joined the confederates to defend slavery. Most tribes were so obliterated with diseases and malnutrition that they were unable more so than unwilling to participate in any more wars.

William W. Brown in his book, "The Black Man" shared a story of a slave who served in the confederate navy named Rober Small in 1862. Robert served on the heavy arm dispatch boat called "The Planter". Due to the laws that govern southern states against integration, and if violated, authorities were permitted to put black sailors in jail and hang them if they stepped foot off their ships while in ports. After a weekend of drunken stupor by the white crew onboard, Robert stole the Planter from its dock, then sailed it into Union waters, where he took down the Stars and Stripes Flag, then replaced it with a white image as a sign of truce. Once in Union jurisdiction, a Union Naval Commander named Samuel F DuPont logged that the steamer (Planter) was a quite valuable acquisition to the squadron by her good machinery and very light draught. When the Planter was refitted as a gunboat by the Union Navy, Robert Small was the mad captain of the war vessel.

The question of should the negro enslaved people be paid, and if so, then how much? Their volunteerism in the war was just that. They receive no monetary payments whatsoever. Luis Emilio, wrote in his book "A Brave Black Regiment" that Lincoln fought with his white hand   while his black hand remained tied: He proclaimed for Men of Color to arm, we can get at the throats of treason through the State of Massachusetts. She was the first in the war of independence, the first to break the chains of her slaves, make the black man equal before the law, and admit color children to her common schools. I need not add more.

Colonial Robert G Shaw wrote in the newspaper, Boston Journal: "Wanted Good men for the Fifty-Fourth Regiment in Massachusetts Volunteers of Negro Descent one hundred bounties by expiration f term of service. Pay thirteen dollars per month, and state aide for families".

Further readings show that the negro soldiers were not paid thirteen dollars per month; they were paid eleven dollars per month, minus three dollars for clothing. The white soldiers received thirteen dollars per month   and stipends for clothing allowances. Those who were against paying negro slaves any monetary benefits cited the "The Massachusetts Milia Act" of 1862, which defined negro slaves as contraband and specified that contrabands would only be paid ten dollars and no alms to their families. Even though the negro slaves fought, killed, and died on the same battlefield as their white counterparts, that did not make a difference.

The question of negro soldiers as Officers was raised. The War Department (Defense Department today) emphatically rejected that idea. And they were micro-specific about maintaining the nine thousand white men they commissioned as officers over negro troops. Conversely, the confederate states branded all negro troops, and the white officers assigned to them as "outlaws." With attrition, and casualties mounting on their side, the confederate military repealed that idea, as they recognized their talents fighting against them was visibly winning. Then, the Confederate armies began recruiting slave men and boys to join the military and possibly free themselves.

One of the bloodiest battles involving negro soldiers was in May 1863, with the siege of Port Hudson in Louisiana. The Union would have controlled the banks of the Mississippi. Although the Union lost that battle; the negro troops won a symbolic victory. James McPherson wrote in his book "The Negros Civil War" the story of Captain Andre Cailloux of the First Louisiana death after he led his troops to battle in open grounds and under heavy artillery fire from the confederates. He was found on the battlefield still crouching his sword. And his last words were "suivez moi" or follow me.

After three days of intense fighting in Vicksburg Mississippi, at Milliken's Bend, the colored troops recorded their firsthand to hand victory over confederate troops. Even though they lost nearly five percent of their troops. In an unbelievable note written by a confederate general named Henry McCulloch saying of the battle "This charge was resisted by the negro portion of the enemy force with considerable obstinacy. The white or pure Yankee portion ran like whipped curs almost as soon as the charge was made". However, it was sergeant William H Carney of the Fifty Fourth Massachusetts to become the first negro recipient of the newly created Medal of Honor. As he was wheeled off the battlefield into the tents of medical assistance, he refused to turn loose the Union flag from his hand.

The black historian William W Brown described in his book "The Black Man" how the negro troops of the First Kansas Volunteer were slaughtered in what is known as the "Fort Pillow Massacre". Fort Pillow was located in Tennessee along the Mississippi River. It was operated by the Eleventh Colored Troops and by white Unionists. In the spring of 1864, Fort Pillow was surrounded by fifteen hundred confederate troops lead by General Nathan B Forrest. After the takeover of Fort Pillow, General Forrest screamed out orders to "take the white men (union soldiers) and to kill the damn niggers, shoot them down." The bodies of the negro soldiers were then set on fire, mutilated, or buried alive. The Mississippi waters covered with crimson; the blood of the massacre colored.

When the Union soldiers sieged, they took control of Fort Fisher in Wilmington North Carolina. The civil war was nearing its end. Fort Fisher was General Lee's Confederate army's most fortified and secured depot. After the fall of Fort Fisher   , Charleston's demise in South Carolina was born months   after that. The confederate depot in Richmond, Virginia, finally met its faith in April 1865. Henry Turner, a chaplain in the First Regiment Colored Troops recorded his account of the battle in the AME Christian Record that now rest in the American Heritage since 1980 that; "at one time I thought they could never stand it, neither do I believe they have stood it, but for the fact that they know the black troops ere in the rear, and if they failed, the colored troops would take the fort and claim the honor. Indeed, the white union troops told the rebels that if they did not surrender, they would let the negroes loose. That threat eventually worked. Because the confederate soldiers surrendered in Richmond Virginia". Dudley Cornish memorializes that battle in his book "The Sable Arms" in a letter written by Colonel Charles France Adams to his father. He wrote, "to have led my regiment, the Fifth Massachusetts Colored Troops into Richmond at the moment of its capture is the one event which I should most have desired as the culmination of my life in the army".

Civilians in the city of Richmond witness-colored soldiers in formation, marching behind the white union soldiers, in victory. They witness negro soldiers arresting and confining white confederate soldiers in defiance. Negro troops were in Appomattox as well, the site where General Robert E Lee surrendered. It was John Wilkes Booth a confederate who foresaw that negro slavery was nearing its final chapter in the south. So, he assassinated President Abraham Lincoln in the Washington Ford Theater, as he watched the "Our American Cousin" James McPherson sort of summarized the final days in his book "The Negros Civil War" like this:

"By the end of the war there were 186,107 Negro enlisted soldiers, or ten to twelve percent of The Union army, and 7,122 were negro officers. There were some 30,000 negro sailors, or eight.

Or twenty-five percent of the Union Navy, with no negro officers. Negro soldiers and sailors had Participated in 449 engagements. At

41

fourteen percent of the population, the Negro male accounted for twenty percent of total Union casualties".

These statistics reflex those negro's who fought and died in the North. I am inclined to believe that similar statistics from the Confederate camp is recorded but must never be published.

The confederates could not get even with the North for losing the war. But they could strike more blows at the heads of the newly released slave property. Historian Sam Dennison wrote in his book song by a capture confederate:

> "O I'm a good ole rebel, now that's just what I am
>
> For this fair land of freedom, I do not care.
>
> I'm glad I fit against it, I only wish'd we won.
>
> And I don't want   any pardon for anything I have done.
>
> I hate the constitution, this great republic too.
>
> I hate the freeman's Buro, In uniforms of blue."

President Lincoln unveils his Emancipation Proclamation in 1863, announcing that "All Men Are Equal". It was a moral and symbolic gesture. But as negro gentry men in both the north and south who fought and died, their families were still living in the bowels of bondage, just unchained. It was the ratification of the Thirteenth Amendment, Section I of 1865 that semi emancipated the negro from slavery:

"Neither slavery nor involuntary servitude, except as a punishment for crime whereof the party shall have been duly convicted shall exist within the United States, or any place subject to their jurisdiction".

From the Thirteenth Amendment came the Fourteenth Amendment Section I of 1868 that says:

> "All persons born or naturalized in the United States, are citizens of the United States and of the State wherein they reside.

It was the valor, dedication, and sacrifice of negro bondsmen who fought, killed, and died on the battlefields that emancipated more than four million slaves from bondage. Their courageousness forced the laws of citizenship for them, their families, and for their descendants. These laws apply to this day, to all refugees, asylee, permanent resident, HB2 visa card holder, or migrant, as a testament from their legacy. Here is what author, and pollical pundit Ann Coulter expressed about these policies. "The biggest scams in immigration law are the humanitarian cases. One hundred percent of refugee and asylum claims are either obvious frauds, or frauds that haven been proved yet. Immigration activists coach immigrants to lie to immigration officials. Document mills produce phony passports, school records, and medical reports. Often asylum applicants know nothing about the country they claim as home. She documents her case in legalistic formants to support her bombastic sentiments. I do not know enough about immigration procedures or immigration laws as the overwhelming number of Americans do not know. But I disagree with many of her inflammatory sentiments regarding immigration.

THE OTHER WILD-WILD WEST
TRAILBLA ZERS

After the final chapters of the civil war, the American colonies made an unrelenting push to conquer the west by exploration, exploitation, treaties, broken treaties, and war against the natives. This war known as the Indian Wars of 1867 would turn out to be different from the previous chapter. The war's enemies had leaders named Geronimo, Lone Wolfe, Sitting Bull, and Crazy Horse. Richard Drinnon highlighted General William T Sherman's first battle cry in his book "Facing West", saying, "we must act with vindication earnestness against the Sioux even to their extermination, men, women and children". Congress in 1866 mandated what was called the "New Army". It read the new army shall consist of five regiments of artillery, ten regiments of calvary, forty-five regiments of infantry, and corps of cadets of the military academy, and other forces as shall be provided by the act". In this new army, congress identified that "to the six regiments of calvary now in service there shall be added fair regiments, two of which shall be composed of colored men, having the same organization as is now provided by law for calvary regiments". Congress also added two new negro infantries' as well. Making one out of every five soldiers a negro man.

Edward Coffman wrote in his book "The Old Army" this statement, "By 1875, the new arm had a permanent strength of about twenty-five thousand civil war veterans, whites and negros formed the New Army's core. But negro troopers stayed longer on the frontier, disserting less and reenlisting more, than their white counterparts. They were also more abstemious, between 1866 and 1885, their ratio of sick calls for drunkenness was only two per one thousand as opposed to the white ration of fifty-four per one thousand.

Negro soldiers in the early western frontier-built thousands of miles of road, and telegraph lines. They escorted stagecoaches, wagon trains, as well as protected homesteaders and ranchers from Indian attacks. They even protected the pony express, or mail from outlaws while on the trails. The negro troops, again served with valor despite being isolated, inferior horses, low artillery supplies, and pay. The army paid negro soldiers thirteen dollars per month. Which was far more money than most recently freed negro civilians who were still sharecroppers, plow horsemen, and domestic workers.

Evan S Connell wrote of the negro soldiers in the Tenth Calvary, in his book "Son of the Morning Star" that "In 1867 when ninety troopers of the Tenth Calvary defeated eight hundred Cheyenne in a two-day battle near Fort Leavenworth, Kansas with a loss of only three cavalryman, black scalps became highly prized. C heyeene called the Tenth Calvary troopers 'Buffalo Soldiers', comparing them to an animal they considered scared. While Indians continued to scalp whites, they later refrained from scalping negros and in fact, did not relish fighting them".

Phillip Drotning wrote in his book, "Black Heroes in Our Nation's History" that it was Emanuel Stance, a sergeant in the Ninth Calvary, that was the first Buffalo Soldier to be awarded the Indian War Metal of Honor". He also wrote, "Leading a detachment of ten troopers at Kickapoo Springs, Texas, he drove off some thirty Kickup's by pulling ahead and repeatedly emptying and reloading his sidearm, without breaking his charge".

Under the Indian Peace Commission of 1867, congress implemented the so-called reservation system as an effort to keep native tribes as far away from western settlers as imaginable. Treaties with the Cheyenne's and Arapahoe were granted almost four million acres of reservation in Oklahoma near the Washia Red River. The Kiowas, Comanche, and Apache tribes receive three million acres. And the government provided them with clothing and food. There are stories written that I read accusing the government of supplying blankets laced with small pots. The natives had no modern immunity against small pots, so they were easily wiped out from the biological weapons used against them.

As the white colonies began encroaching upon the reservations, the Treaties began to be broken. Richard Drinnon wrote in his book "Facing West" that, "In 1867 white arsonists destroyed a village of some one thousand to fifteen thousand Cheyenne and Sioux on the

Pawnee fork of the Arkansas River, hunting grounds guaranteed by government treaty".

When Cheyenne and Arapahoe struck back, the army retaliated. General George Armstrong Custer led a surprise attack on the Washita River encampment of Cheyenne, Chief Black Kettle, indiscriminately killing men, women, children and horses". Eve after the war was over, white settlers not only encroached upon the native territories, but they also burned, pillaged, and conquered the negro territories they established during the Buffalo Soldiers victories on the battlefield. Historians defy the publication of this history. For example, Fort Duchene in Utah, Fort Robinson in Nebraska, Fort Washakie in Wyoming, Fort Tularosa in New Mexico, and fort McKiver in Texas alone the colonist confiscated the Rio Grande borders without any Treaties agreed. Hollywood, and their many motion pictures on the big screens are implicit with this erasure. They portray films featuring cowboys, rodeo's, steer roping, cattle riding, bronco busting, riflemen shooting up the ole corral, Indian slaying bounty hunters.

The Buffalo Soldiers fought in the Spanish American War. It was in February 1898 when the battleship "Maine" exploded while in the harbor in Havana Cuba. The Maine   protected America's interest during the "Cuba Libre", or the Cuban Revolution. That explosion killed two hundred and sixty sailors. Twenty-two of whom were negro sailors. It was the Tenth Calvary of colored troops that answered the call of duty and rescued the famous "Rough Riders" during the war. It was Herschel Cashin who captured this article in his book "Under Fire with The Tenth Calvary":

> "The cowboys always pay their debts,
>
> Them darkies saved us at Hell Caney,
>
> When we go back on the colored vets,
>
> Count Texas Bill out of play. Said the Rough Riders".

Finally, it was Phillip Drotning who once again summarized the Tenth Cavalry heroism in yet another American campaign when he wrote this of Colonel Theodore Roosevelt in 1898:

47

"We went up absolutely intermingled, so that no one could tell whether it was the Rough Riders

Or the men of the Ninth Cavalry who came forward with the greater courage to offer their

Lives in service of their country. When you've been under fire with a man and fought side by

Side with him, and eaten with him when you had anything to eat, and hungered with him when

You hadn't, you felt sort of comradeship that you don't feel for any man that you have been

Associated with in other ways. I don't think that any Rough Rider will ever forget the tie

That binds us to the Ninth and Tenth Cavalry".

The Spanish American Wars of 1898-1917 victories removed the presence of Spanish military forces from the southern hemisphere of America. The victories also opened the doors for trade with Cuba, Puerto Rico, and the Philippines. American military bases were built on all three islands   to protect the trade and political interest of the United States. I believe only one base still remain today. And that is the Naval Base in Guantanamo Bay in Cuba.

THE MILITARY'S DISINFORMATION CAMPAIGN

The Selective Service Act of 1917 mandated that all enlistment of abled bodied men aged twenty-one to thirty-one. Immigration laws set by Congress opened the gates for millions of immigrants to gain citizenship here in America. Primarily from European stock. And those who were not of European descent were classified as whites by default not being negro. They enjoyed all the benefits, perks, privileges, and prosperity that American negro citizens were denied. Byron Farewell wrote in his book "Over There" that foreign born and negroes were over-drafted. By June 85, 1907, more than seven hundred thousand negroes were registered, less than ten percent of the U.S. Population, they made thirteen percent of all U.S. draftee". Of the three hundred sixty-seven thousand, seven hundred and ten negro male draftees, who actually served in the military, eleven percent of that number served in combat. The remainder were assigned to labor, supply, mess hall, and KP duty.

> The beginning of World War I, or the wars in Europe, began on "June 28, 1914, when a Serb nationalist in Sarajevo assassinated Archduke Franz Ferdinand, heir to the Austro-Hungarian throne. The assassin ignited a European chain reaction. All Europe was at war within six weeks, known as a nest of interlocking and opposed understandings and mutual assistance treaties". The Russians supported Serbia, Germany supported Austria, France supported Russia, Britain supported France, and America was neutral. In April of 1917 America entered the war. Roy Wilkins published in his magazine "The Crisis" a letter drafted by General John J Pershings, Headquarters of the American Expeditionary Forces in France that read:

"To the French Military Mission Stationed with The American Army Secret Information Concerning Negro Troops: It is important for French Officers who have been called upon to Exercise command over negro American troops, or live in close contact with them, to have an exact idea of the position occupied by Negroes in the United States...Although a citizen of the United States the negro man is regarded by the whit American as a inferior being with whom relations of business or service only are possible. The negro is constantly being censured for his want of intelligence and discretion, his lack of civic and professional conscience, and for his tendency towards undo familiarity. The vices of the Negro are a constant menace to the American who has to repress them sternly...We must prevent them the rise of any pronounced degree of intimacy between French Officers and negro officers (small case). We may be courteous and amenable with these last　, but we cannot deal with them on the same plane as white American Officers without deeply offending them. We must not eat with them, must not shake hands or seek to talk or meet outside the requirements of military service. We must not commend too highly the negro American troop, particularly in the presence of Americans...Make a point of keeping the native (French) population from spoiling the Negroes. Americans become greatly incensed at any public expression of intimacy between white women and negro men...Familiarity on the part of white women with negro men is furthermore a source of profound regret to our experienced colonial, who see it in an overwhelming menace to the prestige of the white race".

This adhonemous attack was not directed towards any other soldier, sailor, officer, or enlisted in the American armed forces. It was specific in its contents; the negro man must be subjugated by the French military and civilian population as they were back in the States. To their bravery, the French authorities published the article in English so that all the allies had free access to it. By doing this, the German enemy also had access to it. Author, Emmett J Scott recorded one German Theorist, Hans Habe, scenario of the Negro living in America under the rulership of the Third Reich, "Germany would control their jobs and all forms of association that might lead to assimilation. Voting, intermarriage, and access to all public accommodations; including roads, streetcars, and motion pictures would be forbidden under the global Reich. Negros would also be forbidden to serve in the military, except in labor battalion". Roy Wilkins, editor of the "Crisis", wrote that the "Third Reich was already implemented for the American Negro under Jim Crow". The

French authorities had to translate the directive into English, because General Pershings originally wrote it in French.

Author Byron Farewell wrote that "by onset of the war, there were approximately ten thousand negros in the army, all members of the Buffalo Soldiers Nineth and Tenth Calvaries, and Twenty Fourth and Twenty-Fifth Infantries. There were also Ten Thousand negro National Guardsmen, and some ten thousand negro sailors in the Navy. All who were noncombatants in the mess hall on the ships. And all of whom died when their ships were sank by German torpedoes". Not only did General Pershings fear the presence of negro warriors, but so did the Germans. Author   Emett J Scott cited in his book "Official History of the American Negro in the World War" that, "Germans fear of negro troops was confirmed by two captured white American aviators, Lieutenant V. H. Burgin and A.L. Clark. While there were captured at different points, and imprisoned at widely separate prison, both stated that when brought before the German military intelligence department and questioned as to the American forces in France one of the first questions asked of them, and which the Germans seemed most concerned about, was how many-colored troops America had over here. Burgin replied thirteen million. Clark said several million".

Roy Wilkins highlighted another study conducted in 1925 by the Army War College that published this report concerning the negro infantrymen:

"Blacks were physically unqualified for combat duty, because the black brain weighed ten ounces less than the white brain. Blacks, moreover, subservient by nature and believing themselves to be inferior to whites, were susceptible to the influence of crowd psychology and unable to control themselves in the face of danger. Thus, the War Department would not intermingle colored and white enlisted personnel in the same regimental organization. Neither would it assign colored Reserve Officers other than of the Medical Corps and Chaplains to existing black combat units of the regular Army".

Nonetheless, negro American civilians still enlisted in separate service stations, and assigned to segregated army troops. Negro sailors had no option. They were al stuck in the mess hall at the bottom of the ship, preparing and servicing food to the white and other non-black crew. This phenomenon can best be explained by Graham Smith, in his book "When Jim Crow Met John Bull". Here he highlights a speech expressed by late long time Senator Robert Byrd, of West Virginia:

"I am a typical American, a southerner, and 27 years of age, and never in this world will I be convinced that race mixing in any field is good. All the social do gooders, the philanthropic greats of this day, the red and the pinks...the disciples of Eleanor Roosevelt...the pleas by Sinatra...can never alter my convictions on this question...I am loyal to my country and know but reverence to her flag. But I shall never submit to fight beneath that banner with a negro by my side. Rather I should die a thousand times, and see old glory trampled in the dirt never to rise again, than to see this beloved land of ours become degraded by race mongrels, a throwback to the blackest specimens from the wild".

Senator Robert Byrd never volunteered for military service to his country. But his rhetoric against the existence of the negro man match that of General John J Pershing.

THE FIRST TUSKEGEE ACE OF WORLD WAR II

The United States had entered the war of the worlds in Europe to defeat fascism and anti-atrocities against humankind everywhere. In 1941 the Army Department announced the formation of the first negro only Air Corps. The announcement came prior to the threat of lawsuits from Yancy Williams, a Howard University student. He was preparing to sue the Secretary of War for continuously rejecting his Air Corps Cadet training applications. They were called the Ninety-Nineth Pursuit Squadron. It composed of twenty-seven planes, thirty-three officer pilots, and four hundred enlisted men. They were chosen by the Army, using the same criterion used in all non-negro squadrons. The pilot candidates were all college graduates; the enlisted men came from a mechanical background and had college experience. The one-million-dollar Tuskegee Army Airfield was erected in Tuskegee Alabama known as the center of black World War II military aviation. It was led by Charles A "chief" Anderson, and his co-pilot, Albert E Forsythe. Those two were the first negro pilots to complete a transcontinental flight successfully.

The army's experiment was designed to fail from the start. It used the training of single seat pilots, instead of two or more seat aircrews. That would have meant that the army would have had to necessitate all black facilities for bombardiers, navigators, and gunners. Thereby conceding to the idea of separating negro aviators in the same cockpits with white or any other non-aviator race. The second hope for failure was that the Army Department chose Alabama as its experimental site. A southern state with Jim Crow laws that paralyzed its negro citizens from every decent thought of humanity.

The Ninety-Nineth Squadron quickly gave birth to the 332nd Fighter Group, who called themselves "The Red Tails". They derived this name from there red tails pieces on the silver & gray P-51 Mustang planes that they flew. After many air engagements with the German pilots, they called them the "spookwaffe" instead of the Luftwaffe, while some in the American Air Corp nickname them "Eleanor Roosevelts N's".

Jay Maeder, in his book "Fighting Heart, Flip Corakan", a radio operator named John Connel who was a gunner on a B-24 Liberator Bomber described the Red Tails in this manner, "fighter escort duty required taking bombers up to their targets, waiting for them, and returning them to the rendezvous. On a tough raid to Munich, they would have to beat off fierce German attacks, you'd be shooting too. The 332nd was different from other units. You would look out the window off the wing and see your fighter coverage. Ordinarily guys did a certain precision rollover to show you they were friendly, but the Red Tails w would roll that wing over and over and float through the formation like dancers. If you did not know who was in that plane, you knew when you saw them that you were happy. They were that hot, that good. They had class and finesse".

The Red Tails emblem on their flight suit was a fire spitting black panther, over a white star. Lieutenant Lee Archer, a Red Tails pilot , told how the Red Tails were personally requested to escort some B-24 Liberator Bombers. They claimed that white escort pilots from the 15th Air Force Fighters would leave their bombers to chase after Germans in the air, just to get a kill. The punishment for that was court martial, but none of them were ever court martialed or punished.

So, the Red Tails got the orders to escort. In one rendezvous, a B-24 Liberator was hit, and was barely able to cross the Adriatic Sea, it was nursed by Lieutenant Archer to their air stripe. The pilot of that B-24 did not know that the Red Tails were a unit of segregated negro pilots. But the German propagandist called "Axis Sally" knew who the Red Tails were. Over a nazi radio station she named a few of them. There were: Roscoe C Brown, Jr, who became the President of New York City's Bronx Community College. William T Coleman, who afterwards, graduated Harvard Law School, became U.S. Transportation Secretary under President Gerald Ford Administration, and Coleman Young, who later became the Mayor of Detroit.

In 1945 the Red Tails took apart the heavy lead German campaign against the Romania Oil Field at Plosesi, while returning from another mission in Italy. Afterwards, they lead the air attack against the Daimler-Berg tank factory in Berlin Germany on March 24,

1945. Captain Brown, Lieutenant Earl Lane, and their flight officer, Charles Brantly, shot down the smacking brand-new German 262 jet, the Messerschmitt. Captain Brown reported, "we were doing figure eights over the bombers, we escorted, as we flew over Berlin, I notice these streaks above us. They were German jets. We peddled down, then up, then caught one of the 262   s from underneath". The Defense Department used Captain Browns encounter with the Messerschmitts as combat training for new pilots. The Red Tails were created to shout twenty-five enemy planes out of the skies in only two days. They were responsible for the last four enemy kills in the Mediterranean air combat mission. The ir total kills were recorded as one hundred eleven air kills, one hundred fifty planes parked on enemy airfields, and one thousand seventy-five sorties (flight mission) flown.

"MY BLACK MESSIAH"

With his Third Army struggling in the Saar Basin in France, General George S Patton called for the 761st Tank Battalion in Texas. The 761st battalion was one of three segregated Negro battalions   not invited until October 1944. Historians wrote that General Patton loved his tanks.

When the 761st battalion arrived in Europe, they were sent to Omaha Beach in France. It was there when the General first spoke to them. Trezzvant Anderson, in his book "Come Out Fighting" recorded the General's speech to the battalion:

"I don't give a damn what color you are as long as you go up there and kill those, Krauts. You wonder why you're here? I sent for you. Your people are watching you, and by golly, don't let them down, and damn you, don't let them down".

Secured in their Sherman Tanks, with its 76mm gun, weighting thirty tons, and its six-man crew, consisting of its driver, assistant driver, bow gunner, turret gunner, cannoneer, radio operators, and commander. The 761st battalion consisted of thirty black officers, six white officers, and six hundred seventy-six black enlisted men. The 761st battalion was sent as a backup, to assist another battalion bogged down under heavy fire during a German counter-offensive in Hampont and Guebling. Once in battle, the 761st was responsible for more than three hundred German soldiers' deaths. Staff Sergeant Ruben Rivers of Tecumseh Oklahoma got out of his tank, while under fire, and removed German roadblocks that prevented the tanks from moving forward. Staff Sergeant Rivers head was blown off by German artillery. His family was awarded the Silver Star in his honor, for his heroism. General Frasier, in his book "Book recalls Black World War II Tank Battalion" wrote that "David Williams II, a white Captain in the 761st, who was a young punk out of Yale, who knew no negroes except for the family main and their chauffeur and considered me a most unlikely candidate for negro troops. But I got my manhood with them. These guys were better than heroes because they weren't supposed to be able to fight, and they are treated like lepers. I can tell you; it took a rare sort of character to go out there and do what they do. I ask myself, why the hell should these guys fight? Why"?

The 761st fought across France, Belgium, Luxembourg, and Germany. Their mission was to join up with the Soviet Union forces as they fought their way across Eastern Europe, Poland, and Czechoslovakia. As the 761st approached Austria, they camped across what they thought was a satellite camp at Gunskirchen, which turned out to be a camp set up by the Germans to house thousands of European Jews.

Members of the 761st said they thought the camp was a German housing unit or barracks. But as they buttoned down for battle, they saw people with heads clean, in strip suits, many hanging out of windows, people that looked like white ghosts, skeletons with skin wrapped around them, just walking and wandering around. Then, inside the camp, some bodies looked like skin and bones all around the barracks. What the hell is this? This was one of the Germans concentration camps. When the 761st arrive   d to assist, white infantrymen were already there providing care. So, they continued to travel to Austria to meet up with the Russians. They passed another concentration camp in Mauthausen, where they just viewed the scenery with awe. This time the 761st recognized what was in front of them, evidence of the Holocaust.

The 761st tank battalion was disbanded as the war ended in May 1945. Before their return to America, battalion members told stories of how they had to stand behind German and Italian POWs in the mess hall so that they could eat before them, and how they were not allowed to attend concerts hosted by the United Service Office (USO).

When Hollywood aired the movie Paton in the 1970's, none of the Tuskegee air group pilots or members of the 761st tank battalion were shown in the film. Instead, there was one Negro man that made an appearance, and he was General Paton's orderly.

Nonetheless, one young survivor rescued from the Mauthausen concentration camp who grew up in America recognized her rescuer. Her name was Sonia Schreiber Weitz.   She wrote the following of her heroes in her memoirs: "I was 15 years old when I arrived at Mauthausen. I survived the ghetto in Cracow Poland and various death camps, including Auschwitz and Bergen Belsen. We finally got to Mauthausen, the same camp where my father and Norbert was taken; Norbert survived, but my father was killed. We were six on a bunk like sardines. The allies knew what was happening to us by 1942; but we were not a priority. They refused to bomb the railroad tracks which took u to Auschwitz. I remember one day, there was a negro American soldier. This particular negro that I remembered was standing there totally devastated by what he saw. The horror on his face is something that, even in my state, I cannot ever forget. I weighed about sixty pounds and was really more dead than alive.

I will conclude my presentation with this poem I call, "A Black Messiah Came for Me":

A Black GI stood by the door I never saw a Black before

He set me free before I died, I thought, he must be the Messiah.

A Black Messiah came for me...He stared with eyes that didn't see.

He never heard a single word which hung absurd upon my tongue.

And then he simply froze in place The shock, the horror on his face.

He didn't weep, he didn't cry but deep within his gentle eyes...

A flood of devastating pain, his innocence forever stained.

For me, with yet another down, I found my black Messiah gone.

And on we went our separate ways for many years without a trace.

But there's a special bond we share, which has grown because we dare.

To live, to hope, to smile...and yet, we vow not ever to forget'.

Robert Fikes, a contributor, wrote in his article in "Black Past", this story about a negro man name Milton Wright. He writes "The only person of negro descent known to have had a face-to-face conversation with the infamous Nazi Fuhrer Adolf Hitler was the economist Milton Samuel Wright. He was born in Savannah, Georgia, on June 28, 1903, the son of William Wright and Edith Burnside Wright. William received a bachelor's degree from Wilberforce University in Ohio, then a master's from Columbia University in 1928. Like a handful of negro Americans who found graduate study in pre-World War II Europe intellectually challenging. Wright pursued his Doctorates in Economics at the prestigious University of Heidelbert, founded in 1386. As a student leader he had earlier been invited to attend international student conferences at the University of Cologne in Germany and Oxford University in England. From there, he made efforts to launch a student exchange program between historically black institutions in the U.S. and German Universities.

In Heidelberg in the summer of 1932, after viewing a regional political rally with some German friends and hearing a typically demagogic speech by Adolf Hitler, Wright had the misfortune of being overheard joking to his friends that he would be willing to assassinate the future dictator. SS Guards accosted him as he approached a restaurant in the Europaischer hof Hotel in Heidelberg where, coincidentally, Hitler was staying and had ordered Wright to be brought to him.

Wright, fluent in German, and well aware of nazi ideology, entered Hitlers room with extreme trepidation and feared he might not leave alive. As recounted years later in the Pittsburgh Courier, and in Ebony Magazine, that was founded by John H Johnson in 1945 with his publishing company in Chicago Illinois, (Ebony magazine today is owned and operated by foreign publisher's who have tabloid the magazine to the brink of insolvency). Their conversation, which was pretty much a one-way affair with Hitler asking, then answering his own questions to Wright in a calm but rather loud voice. Though indicating to some extent, he was aware of the history of negroes (in America) and that he respected Booker T Washington and Paul Robeson. Hitler, less than six months away from becoming Chancellor of Germany, nonetheless asserted educated negroes like Wright were certain to be miserable because they were forever destined to be third-class people, cowardly slaves, and mere imitators of superior races. Your people are a hopeless lot. I don't hate them, he said, "I pity the poor devils. Wright's ordeal lasted four hours but Hitler had been surprisingly courteous, had complimented Wright's excellence in the German language, and suggested they meet for another session in Munich, and gave Wright an autographed photo of himself as a memento. Wright returned to America and resumed employment at Samuel Huston College in Austin Texas. He married the former Sue H Hurt. For nearly four decades Wright taught and was an administrator at Wilberforce where he retired in 1969 as Professor of Economics and Political Science and Vice President for Research".

In conclusion, what this Survivor may not have known, is that the German regime were oppressors of other nations long before Auschwitz. John Lewis-Stempel write about their invasion, and colonization of the small country of Namibia in 1885 when German troops were defeated by the indigenous Herero tribesmen who revolted against German soldiers over seizure of their land. "After beating the Herero force in the battle of Waterberg, the German drove the survivors into the pitiless Omaheke desert with the intention they should die from thirst and starvation. Water Holes were poisoned by cleansing patrols of the Schulztruppe, the colonial army, to prevent the Herero from using them. The natives were rounded up, put on cattle wagons, and sent by trains to

"KONZENTRATIONSLAGERS" concentration camps where they were brutalized, and starves as slave laborers. The estimated Herero population was reduced from nearly eighty thousand to fifteen thousand. And of the Nama Tribe; from about twenty thousand to less than ten thousand survivors". The atrocious acts were photographed by the Germans using kodak roll film cameras, then sent back to Germany as pornographic postcards. In Berlin the German general staff publicly lauded Trotha for his extermination measures.

WHEN THE "SAMURAI" ATTACKED

When the Japanese Imperial Navy conducted an unprovoked aerial attack on the U.S. Pacific Fleet in Pearl Harbor Hawaii on December 7, 1941, in their effort to regain control of the Pacific Islands, and their determination to take control over China, there was no time to react to the onslaught. As Japanese bombers targeted the USS West Virginia, there was one mess-hall worker named Dorie Miller, a son of sharecroppers from Waco Texas, who rushed from the bows of the ship and manned one of the ships fifty caliber anti-aircraft Gatlin guns and managed to shoot down four elite Japanese Naka-Jima Kate Bombers. But the Pentagon gave him credit for only two kills, even though eyewitnesses testified that it was four kills. Dorie then sprinted up to the bridge, then to the captains' quarters, where he assisted white sailors rendering aide to the ship's commander, as they carried him to safety. It was only when West Virginia began to sink, did Dorie abandon ship to save his own life.

Seaman Dorie Miller could have been court-martial for his heroics. At that time, it was against Navy Regulations for a negro sailor to be trained on the use of ammunition onboard American warships. Negro sailors in the Navy could not be segregated at sea like their fellow soldiers in the Army, or pilots in the Air Force. So, they were stationed at the bottom of the ship where they cooked, swabbed the decks, or painted the hulls. They were never allowed topside. The Coast Guards adopted the same regulations the Navy did on their vessels. The Marine Corps were not accepting negro recruits at that time, so no directives for segregation were ever implemented for that branch.

Dorie Miller was the first American Hero of the war in the pacific. However, Doris Goodwin in her book "No Ordinary Time" wrote "The first Navy dispatches from Pearl Harbor described him as an unidentified negro messman". Reluctant to acknowledge the first hero of the was a negro, the Navy Department gave that title to a white hero named Colin Kelly, a captain in the Navy who crash dived his plain into the hull of a Japanese battleship two days after the Pacific Fleet began to engage the Japanese Navy. Dorie was not taken away from the war to participate in 'hero's day parades' to heighten patriotism back home, and to help raise war bonds like white servicemen were. However, five months after Dori herbalism in Pearl Harbor, the military awarded him the Navy Cross. It was presented to him by Admiral Chester W Nimitz, Commander of the U.S. Pacific Fleet. That was the highest decoration for valor in combat. Dorie Miller was killed on Thanksgiving Day in 1943 when a Japanese torpedo sank the aircraft carrier USS Liscome Bay. Dorie died at sea, still a kitchen worker. Some thirty years later, President Richard M Nixon broke ground, and commissioned the USS Dorie Miller, a fast frigate in his honor in June 1973. But it was an earlier mess-hall worker by the name of Leonard Roy Harmon, another son of sharecroppers from Cuero Texas, onboard the cruiser USS Tuscaloosa that received the prestigious Navy Cross when he died rescuing shipmates' topside who were struck by Japanese projectiles during the battle of Guadal-Canal (even though his presence topside was against Navy Regulations). The USS Harmon (DE 678) was commissioned in 1943 to honor him. And the HMS Alymer, in the British fleet, was briefly named the Harmon.

Just like in World War I, no negros in World War II were awarded the Medal of Honor. Acts of negro heroism, except the most undeniably extraordinary, were always overlooked, not by white commanders on the battlefields, who were often surprisingly fair about frontline medal recommendations for them, but by their superior officers who usually filed the recommendations in wastebaskets. But later to be revisited by future Presidents long after the death of the patriots.

EXECUTIVE ORDER-9981

The United States entered the Korean War in June 1950. That campaign was basically known to military historians as a United Nations issue, and conflict. It began when the North Korean Army troops invaded the Thirty-Eighth Parallel into South Korea and began to attack.

President Harry S Trueman at the time, was reluctant to involve American troops, so he ordered air support for the South Koreans. And then he sent the Navy's Seventh Fleet, from the Straits of Taiwan, as a show of force only. Then President Trueman began worrying about the surge of Communist Soviet Union and Communist China influence and support of the North Koreans, as U.S. ground troops began to arrive. However, air power was the catalyst of this war, coinciding with armor tank battalions.

Studying this campaign brought me to a hometown hero named Daniel "Chappie" James, Jr. He became the first negro full four-star general in American history. James grew up near the Naval Air Base in Pensacola and was in awe of war planes he saw flying in the skies over his neighborhood. He eventually became a civilian pilot and teacher, while awaiting to be admitted to the Air Force Tuskegee Institute in Birmingham. Because of his height, and weight, he was too large to fit comfortably in the cockpits of a fighter or first attack plane. So, he was assigned to al negro Four Seventy-Seventh Bombardment Group which was activated in 1944. James petitioned to join a unified group to show the Air Force that he was not just a good bomber in a segregated air group, but a great bombardier in any squadron, including unified ones. I stress unified squadrons, battalions, and troops, because non-negro Americans, during this time, were by default, considered to be white Americans.

In 1949 Chappie James got his opportunity to shine. He was assigned to the Twelfth Fighter Bomber Squadron at Clark Fields in the Philippines. He, and his family received tremendous hostilities on the base merely because of their race. His flying ability was unmatched. He ranked first in rocketry, second in bombing accuracy, and was amongst the top ground gunners in the squadron. When the Twelfth Fighter bomber Squadron was called to enter the war in Korea, the Koreans choice met them, P-15 Mustangs in the air and by the Russian-made F-34 tanks on the ground. While providing air coverage in Nam Chon Jom in North Korea, James flew strikes after strikes after strikes until he ran out of ammunition. He alone was responsible for hundreds of enemy casualties. He was awarded the Distinguished Flying Cross in that encounter. He was later awarded the Distinguished Service Medal for pulling a white pilot from the runway after a jet crash. During that rescue, he suffered a fractured vertebrae and multiple burns on his body.

Author, Peter Bergman described the following of James: "During the Korean War, China entered the battle, and brought with them the Russian made MIG's fighter planes. By that time, Chappie was flying jets. He was shot down by Korean gunners flying a reconnaissance mission. As he catapulted out of his jet behind enemy lines, to his auspicious, he was rescued by an all-white Marine Corp tank crew who had broken through enemy lines prior to his ejection".

Throughout the Korean war, Chappie James was credited for one hundred combat missions. And became the first black officer to train pilots on their way to war. And in 1953, he Commanded the first integrated Air force Fighter Squadron in America. In his honor, the State of Florida named the Daniel "Chappie" James, Jr, building after him. Another bitter, but sweet coincidence occurred after the Korean War. With the signing of Executive Order-9981 in 1948 by President Harry S Truman, eventually ended the practice of maintaining segregated units in the armed forces of America. A brief history of that order is as followed:

In 1940, Black Americans made up almost 10 percent of the total U.S. population (12.6 million people out of a total population of 131 million). Of the 2.5 million Black-American males who registered for the draft through December 31, 1945, more than one million were inducted into the armed forces. These inductees served in all branches of service and in all Theaters of Operations during World War II.

During World War II, President Roosevelt had responded to complaints about discrimination at home against Black Americans by issuing Executive Order 8802 in June 1941. It directed that Black Americans be accepted into job-training programs (where they were historically shut out of, especially in the south) in defense plants, forbid discrimination by defense contractors, and established a Fair Employment Practices Commission (FEPC).

After the war, President Harry Truman, Roosevelt's successor, faced a multitude of problems and allowed Congress to terminate the FEPC. However, in December 1946, Truman appointed a distinguished panel to serve as the President's Commission on Civil Rights, which recommended "more adequate means and procedures for the protection of the civil rights of the people of the United States." When the commission issued its report, "To Secure These Rights," in October 1947, among its proposals were anti-lynching and anti-poll tax laws, a permanent FEPC, and strengthening the civil rights division of the Department of Justice.

In February 1948, President Truman called on Congress to enact all of these recommendations. When Southern Senators (from both sides of the political spectrum) immediately threatened a filibuster, Truman moved ahead on civil rights by using his executive powers. Among other things, Truman bolstered the civil rights division, appointed the first Black American judge to the Federal bench, and named several other African-Americans to high-ranking administration positions. And on July 26, 1948, he issued this executive order abolishing segregation in the armed forces and ordering full integration of all branches.

Executive Order 9981 stated that "there shall be equality of treatment and opportunity for all persons in the armed forces without regard to race, color, religion, or national origin." It established the President's Committee on Equality of Treatment and Opportunity in the Armed Services to recommend revisions to military regulations in order to implement this policy.

The advisory committee examined the rules, practices, and procedures of the armed services and recommended ways to make desegregation a reality. The committee, chaired by Charles Fahy, was terminated upon submission of its final report, entitled "Freedom to Serve," on May 22, 1950.

There was considerable resistance to the executive order from the military, but by the end of the Korean conflict, almost all of the military was integrated.

With the signing of Executive Order 9981 it, unfortunately, dismantled the historical history of the Tuskegee Air Institute where only negro pilots were trained. It also dismantled the historical 761st Tank Battalion formerly known as the Buffalo Soldiers. Also, the Order stipulates discrimination against race, color, religion, and national origins. When in practice, since the Revolutionary War in 1770, and every other military campaign that followed. Segregation only separated one race of soldiers, sailors, and airmen serving on the same battlefields, the Negro!

Having separate forces fighting under the same flag meant that those soldiers who were deemed not appropriate to fight alongside the general forces were at a suicidal disadvantage. They were sent to war as guinea pigs. They had less training, less supplies, less medical support, less ammunition, less artillery, less food, and less communication to call for backup. However, those victors still fought and overcame many obstacles on the battlefield. And they lost a great deal more as well.

Some campaigns followed the signing of Executive Order 9981 such as the Vietnam War, Operation Desert Storm and so forth. However, mandatory segregation of the Armed Forces was dismantled under this Executive. Nonetheless, Executive Orders are customarily not enacted upon by incoming Presidents. I am not aware whether Congress has ever voted on this Order into law, or if it still exists as an Executive Order. If so, then it can be reinstituted into practice at any given time.

I quote the concise words of our legendary singer Smokey Robinson reciting his poem on the daytime talk show "The View", to the chagrin of the cast. He said, "To the wonderful Black Americans who served in the Armed Forces and gave their lives in all the wars. They did not do that for Timbuktu, Cape Town, or

Kenya. They did that for Mississippi, Alabama, Georgia, Louisiana, Texas, and Virgina".

Enough of these mythical marvel stories of fictitious villages of warriors, in Wakanda, coming to America. We have our own defenders to celebrate INCONUS. These are the people our Forty-Fifth President honored in his speech on October 4, 2019, in Washington D.C.

THE PUBLIC ACCOMMODATIONS ACT

I once asked a Judge who was teaching a course I was in as an undergraduate, what is an Act? His reply was so legalistic that I was more confused than I was prior to asking the question. He did not answer my question overtly, but he hinted where it was. I found the answer before his lecture was over. The definition was in one of our textbooks required for that class. It said "an alternative name for statutory law. After enacting the terms law and act may be used interchangeably, introduced with the words "Be it enacted instead of Be it resolved".

This Civil Rights Bill I want to discuss was initially called "Public Law 88-352-July 1964". It simply state:

To enforce the constitutional right to vote, to confer jurisdiction upon the district courts of the United States to provide injunctive relief against discrimination in public accommodations, to authorize the Attorney General to institute suits to protect constitutional rights in public facilities and public education. To prevent discrimination in federally assisted programs. Be it enacted by the Senate and House of Representatives of the United States of America in Congress assembled, that this Act may be cited as the "Civil Rights Act of 1964".

I turned my attention to two catchy political phrases our nation is bombarded with every four years during our presidential elections, "Voting Rights". After the civil war, congress added voting rights to the U.S. Constitution as its Fifteenth Amendment in 1870. That announce that the once negro male-slave via the draft, now has permission to vote for primarily white male and a sprinkle of white female candidates running for public positions. The word privilege is used instead of rights, because the Fifteenth Amendment did not prevent State Statues in the south to undo the rights or privileges pertaining to negros.

Author, David Barton in his book "American History", described nine legislations that disenfranchised negros from participating in the election of candidates of their choice:

Poll Taxes: This required the voter to pay an arbitrary fee at the polls before they could vote. Poor whites and all other non negro were also affected by pool taxes. But remember, the tax was arbitrary and was only applied to the negro by white poll workers.

Literacy tests: The pollsters would ask the negro voters questions like, how many pebbles are in this jar, name the Bill of Rights under ten seconds, how many bubbles are in this bar of soap. This too affected poor whites, but it eliminated all the negros.

Grandfather clause: This granted only voters whose father, or grandfathers were registered voters prior to the Fifteenth Amendment. This practice eliminated negros permanently from participation.

Suppressive election procedures: Pollsters would move poll stations without notifying negro voters, or armed guards would be posted outside polling stations where they would threaten and harass negros away. Other times, the pollsters would simply disqualify the ballots of every negro who cast one.

Black codes: Since 1865 measures made into law prevented negros from holding office, owning property, serving on juries, testifying against any white person for whatever reason, owning firearms, including knives in the public, forming segregated armies unless white officers were in charge, and from voting.

Gerrymandering: Legislatures would craft negro districts to include white district so large in populations, that ensuring that no negro candidate would win, even in their own heavily populated district, they would have a white representative.

Whites only primaries: Elections only white voters were allowed to vote. It was fair, because only white candidates were allowed to campaign. Michael Klarman describes this phenomenon in more detail in his book "The White Primaries".

Violence: Lynchings, dismemberment, or threats thereof was successful in preventing negros from participating in voting.

Criminalization: Lawmakers would over nightly institute laws such as loitering, vagrancy, or talking back to a white person that criminalized negros, thereby stripping away any privileges negros had. The Voting Rights Act states:

"Be it enacted by the Senate and House of representatives of the United States of America in Congress assembled, that this Act may be cited as the 'Civil Rights Act of 1964'.

No person acting under the color of law shall in determining whether any individual is qualified under State law or laws to vote in any Federal election, apply any standard, practice or procedures different from standard, practice, or procedures to other individuals within the same county, parish, to be qualified to vote.

Deny the right of any individual to vote in any Federal election because of an error or omission on any record or paper relating to any application, registration, or any other act requisite to voting.

Employ any literacy test as a qualification for voting in any Federal election unless, such test is administered to each individual and is conducted wholly in writing, such tests for persons who are blind or otherwise handicapped meets the purpose, the phrase 'literacy test' includes any test of the ability to read, write, understand, or interpret any matter".

What is disturbing about this Act is that the group of people who were specifically targeted to disenfranchised (Negros) are not even mentioned in the law. Instead, phrases like "any individual", or "each individual" are substituted. That protection includes every group of voters, then and now.

As you see the Bill was placed under the Civil Rights Acts of 1964. That Act was originally called the Public Accommodations Act, but then changed by Congress to read the Civil Rights Act. Here, we have another Bill addressing everyone; then, and now, but not redressing the descendants of the group that paid the ultimate and unnecessary sacrifices, often with their lives, the American Negro.

Today, there is a rush by current social justice groups who have targeted the American experience of my ancestors to coexist with their platform. They attempt to Diversify, Inter-Sectionalize, and Equify their agenda as the same. They come as komisars, cosplayers, and political muckrakers. They stage disorderly campus tours using politicians, entertainers, academia, and many other surrogates to bolster their agenda.

They microphone how critical it is to further black history, as they quietly sprinkle in their motive operandi to hijack it with their rhetoric. But that tactic is harmed when states like Florida already instituted provisions to mandate black history, along with other international experiences. Florida Statute 1003. (1)(h) states "Each district school board shall provide all courses required for middle grades promotion, high school graduation, and appropriate instruction designed to ensure that reading and other language arts, mathematics, science, social studies, foreign languages, health and physical education, and the arts. The history of Black Americans, the enslavement experience, abolition, and the history and their contributions".

"WHEN AFFIRMATIVE ACTION WAS WHITE"

It was the creation of the Selective Service Readjustment Act of 1944 which is known today as the GI Bill that started suburbs in the middle 1900's. Michael Bennett, in his book "When Dreams", described the Act as "The GI bill changed where and how Americans lived. Suburbs sprained up like mushrooms around every sizable city. As surely as the Homestead Act of 1862 filled the prairies of the far west, the GI Bill created and filled the suburbs".

According to Helen Horowitz, in her book "Campus Life", by 1955 about 2,250,000 veterans participated in higher education. The country gained more than 400,000 engineers, 200,000 teachers, 90,000 scientists, 60,000 doctors, and 20,000 dentists". Another 5,600,000 veterans enrolled in various vocational institutions earning degrees in trades such as plumbing, HVAC electrician, and automobile mechanics.

The GI Bill also allowed for business loans from participating banks, job placement assistance, as well as subsidizing mortgages. From this Bill, the Veterans Administration was created.

Black servicemen were also guaranteed the same benefits and protections that all others are since it was a federal backed program. According to Michael Brown, of the Research Division, Coordinated Service, Veterans Administration revealed that fifty-one percent of black veterans had participated in more than one GI Bill program. However, the sample size was small, and the majority of those veterans may have lived in the north, opposed to the south. Where Jim & Jane Crow laws overwhelmingly stranglehold black veterans from the program's full benefits packages.

It was the actions of Mississippi's Representative John Rankins, Chairman of the Committee on World War Legislation, that drafted laws that took the federal run GI Bill away from the Federal Government control, into State control and to local district offices to administer the program as they saw fit. Chairman Rankins fought assertively to make Jim Crow safe. He feared any threat to segregation. "He keenly grasped that negro veterans would attempt to use their new status, based on service to country, and sacrifice, along with a new body of federal funds, to shift the balance against segregation. Given the comparatively young age of the negro population in the South, a significant proportion of Negro men would be returning home after military service far more ready than before to assert their rights and claim their due". The Chairman went on to say, "The difficulties of the Negro veteran are not the same as those of any other minority group of ex-servicemen for the simple reason that all other minorities are considered as being white, and with but few isolated exceptions are treated as such".

The segregated south administered the program so disproportionately and in favor of white GI's, and against black GI's that Kathleen Frydl wrote in her book "GI Bill", that "flexibility that enabled discrimination against black veterans also worked to the advantage of many other veterans". This aspect of affirmative action for whites, the path of job placement, loans, unemployment benefits, schooling tied to the VA Centers, local banks denying mortgage and education loans to black GI's, even though the GI Bill backed them, place southern black service members exactly where John Rankins intended. At the sole mercy of America's Jim & Jane Crow practice of marginalizing the wealth, education, and freedom to exercise their own destiny as die every other non-black veteran in America.

Black servicemen were denied on-the-spot training for skills they learned prior to the military, or during their time in service. However, if their military skills were in cooking, or porter work more times than not they receive job placements. Thereby maintaining the whites only enrollment in trade schools promising future jobs in small engine repair to universities teaching law, or medicine. Reuben Thompson highlighted in his book "Critical Aspects" that the southern strategy brilliantly in action, in his conclusion of the State of Virginia GI Bill run program, where it was written that The State of Virginia does not intend to provide equal opportunities for higher education of Negroes in the near future; if at all"! So, the universal practice at that time was to weaponize government programs to assist and advance every community in America, which it achieved. But to set back the progression of Negro communities, which it also achieved.

Still living in a world of segregation that had been sanctioned by the "separate but equal" doctrine the Supreme Court had applied in 1896 in Plessy v Ferguson upholding a Louisiana law that required separate railway cars for whites and everyone else, with the exception of the Negros. Seventeen southern states stipulated separate schools at all levels. White and colored persons shall not be taught in the same school, the Virginia Codes of 1928 and 1942 instructed. Tennessee law declared: It shall be unlawful for any school, academy, college, or other place of learning to allow white and colored persons to attend the same school, academy, college or other place of learning. Mississippi's constitution was amended in 1942 and 1944 to specify which colleges were open to whites and which to negros. Pauli Murray wrote, "for example, the state's code identified the purpose of the Mississippi State College for White Women as the moral and intellectual advancement of the white girls of the State. In contrast, Alcorn Agricultural and Mechanical college existed for the education of the colored youth of the state. The core opportunity for Negro veterans thus lay with black institutions. Seventeen of these colleges had been founded under the Second Morrill Act of 1890, which disallowed federal support to states if they did not create separate schools for negros when other state colleges excluded them.

The pressure that veterans exerted on black institutions helped enlarge their curricula, which traditionally had been limited to education, theology, and various trades. Here the law's financial provisions did open doors where previously they had been closed by States supporting Jim Crow. And those lucky enough to find a place had a much better chance at middle class status than those who did not. As a result, the GI Bill exacerbated rather than narrowed the economic and educational differences between negros and all other citizens" according to a study titled "Closing Gap".

I have a family member who was drafted into the Vietnam War. He used his GI Bill to complete two different apprenticeship programs, and to purchase his first home for his wife and four children. They were able to relocate to a nicer area in New Orleans where they all flourished. I personally used my veteran status to assist me; a little, with my college tuition and education and to purchase my first home. To this day, I have veteran perks that are available to me via the Veterans Office.

Speaking of government programs, Political Scientist & History Professor Ira Katznelson looked at the early history of affirmative action from the New Deal to Lyndon Johnson's Great Society in his book titled "When Affirmative Action Was White", the title I chose for this chapter. He spoke on the ear of the welfare state that America was changing into. At the time of the Great Depression and minimum paying jobs, hurting families turned to their political representatives to involve the national government to take the lead with programs that can provide them with assistance.

He wrote about three federal programs introduced and passed by congress designed to curtail poverty in America known as the "New Deal". The first was Aid to Dependent Children (ADC), The ADC Program was designed to provide grants to families with young children raised by single parents. Usually meaning the father was absent from the home. The second was the Social Security Act of 1935. That program was designed to provide monetary monthly assistance to the elderly, poor, and to widows of old age. The crux of the Social Security payments was to be derived from the recipient's prior work history and wages. The third tier of the New Deal was the Unemployment Compensation Act. This program provided monetary payments to unemployed workers whose employers made payments into the unemployment insurance fund. However, the southern strategy in congress saw fit to highjack the initiatives away from the federal government and to place them in the hands of the States where they fed Jim Crowe by widening the gap between the Negro and every other American by tinkering with the eligibility requirements for each program. They were able to disqualify jobs such as sharecropping, farm workers, and housekeeping as ineligible for social security work credits. At that time, Negros on a large scale was the sector of American society who was hired to perform agrarian style work. But they were ineligible for social security benefits because they were not earning work credits. They were also not eligible for unemployment benefits because those employers were not obligated by law to pay into their unemployment fund. The same impediments were implemented for the ADC programs.

Richard Sterner, a demographer, showed the disparities between whites and negros in his book "Negro Share". He wrote "in considering the situation in Georgia of the nearly twenty-four thousand whites eligible for aid in 1935, fourteen-point four percent were on the State's roll. Whereas out of the twenty-three thousand negros eligible for aid in 1935, only a mere on point five percent were on the rolls. He concluded that the fact remains that Negro children in Georgia have scarcely benefited from aid to dependent children and have suffered more than white children from the inadequacies of the existing program".

Another Political Scientist name Robert Lieberman described the Negro condition in his book "Shifting the Color Line" that discrimination by means of race-laden provisions with the capacity and intent to divide the population along racial lines without saying so in many words". Negro Americans participation into social security was more dismal than its participation in ADC Gunnar Myrdal, a Swedish Sociologist who lived in Georgia described in his book "An American Dilemma" that social security provided against the hazards of old age at a time when more than one half of negro men, compared with one half of white men remained in the labor market after the age of seventy-fiver. It insured against unemployment when twenty-six percent of negro men and thirty-two percent of negro women were out of work, compared to eighteen percent of white men, and twenty four percent of white women". The Act signed into law by President Roosevelt had clauses that specifically stated, "we opposed exclusions of any specific industries within these Federal Act". It also recommended mandatory inclusion of all workers earning two hundred fifty dollars per month, including agricultural workers, domestic servants, home workers, and many self-employed people under the new landmark law passed in the 1940's".

It was not until the wave of Republican victories in Congress in 1954 when southern democrats were defeated, that the occupational exclusions enacted by the Dixiecrats was eliminated. And even then, negro families did not begin to elevate their status because the Social Security Act stipulated that the wage earner must have at least five years of creditable work credits. Today it stipulates that the wage earner needs ten years of creditable work credits to be eligible for retirement benefits.

In its inception, the New Deal Programs did little to nothing to support the poverty-stricken families in the Negro communities compared to those of other communities. Even the once allies of the cause, the NAACP and the Urban League rejected President Roosevelt's New Deal saying, "it is like a sieve with holes in it just big enough for the majority of Negroes to fall through".

The close of the Nineteen Sixties marked our nation's first civil rights laws (I believe the proper name should have been Human Rights laws). It also left behind some of the melancholy memories. The images of the violent use of force tactics by local authorities supported by the States under Jim Crow against unarmed, peaceful marchers who were dressed in their Sunday's best, holding signs, and singing songs, exercising their rights to do so in public space. The beatings in the streets by gestapo gear police forces with their trained K-9 enforcers turned loose. Being hosed down like burning rubble by fire-fighters in front of the cameras. The frivolous arrest charges levied against the marchers.

Scenes like George Wallace, the Governor of Alabama, surrounded by armed National Guardsmen, blocking the doorway so that elementary school aged negro children could not enter. The open contempt for educational opportunities traces back to the service academies in the 1800's. Take the story of Lieutenant Carl T Rowan, he was the only negro among three hundred four white pilots in training to fly the new V-12 plane. He wrote in his book "Breaking Barriers, "It opened new horizons of opportunity and potential achievement. Rowan's white roommate quipped that he was too busy trying to pass the physics course to count the pigment of his skin. The Commander of the V-12 training program commended Rowan for his icy stare with which he handled overt bigotry. Rowan was then transferred to Northwestern University to train in 1944 but the university refused to permit a negro to live on campus. So, he was sent to the Oberlin College program where he completed the program.

To the enactment of the Morrill Act of 1880. Even to the race base disqualification of negro applicants such as the story of Marion Hood. His story was re-published in the Atlanta Journal-Constitution by Ernie Suggs. He writes, "throughout American history Doctor Hood and so many other talented students were denied access to achieve their dreams to realize their potential. Hood, 83 years old said 'he never dwelled on rejection, The Emory deal in itself was good, to bring some closure. Discrimination to me was an everyday part of life'. The article then posted the denial letter that Doctor Hood kept. It read, "I am sorry I must write you that we are not authorized to consider for admission a member of the Negro race. I regret that we cannot help you. I am returning herewith your $5.00 application fee". The letter was dated August 5, 1959.

Although many of America's vibrant colleges and universities were built by the hands of the people who never receive closure for their forced, free labor, the Morrill Act still must exist.

We saw President John F Kennedy assassination in 1963 in Dallas Texas. Then his brother Rober F Kennedy was assassination in 1968 in Los Angeles California. Then the Reverend, Doctor Martin L King was assassination in 1968 in Memphis Tennessee. To this day our nation still honors those victors, and many others.

There were threats made from the "Peoples House" in congress such as this one from the late segregationist Senator Jesse Helms, (R), North Carolina against the peaceful March on Washington when he said: "The Negro cannot count forever on the kind of restraint that's thus far left him free to clog the streets, disrupt traffic, and interfere with other men's rights".

However, regarding Reverend King, his assassination was not the first attempt on his life. The one time he visited New York in 1958 a woman named Izola Curry pulled a seven-inch steel letter opener out of her purse and stabbed him in his chest as he was signing autographs in Harlem. The authorities in New York reported that Izola also stashed a 25-caliber pistol in her bra. Medical X-rays showed that the tip of the blade was on the edge of his aorta, his main artery.

But the act that captured the memory of this icon was the action of Kadie Hall. Congresswoman Kadie B Hall, (D) was one of twelve siblings from Mississippi. She was first elected to Congress from the Ninety-Seventh District in Indiana in 1981. She sponsored H.R. 3706. The Bill that would make the birthdate of Doctor King a national holiday. Not only did she sponsor the Bill, but she argued it on the floor of the U.S. House of Representatives. When the Bill was sent to the other Chamber, it was the lone Senator from Arizona, John McCain (R) who filibustered it. The Bill was eventually Passed, then signed into law by President Ronald Reagan in 1983.

But I remember a condescending remark from a classmate. She said she does not celebrate or recognize King's Day because she was not an American. She was Caribbean (her family immigrated from Guyana). We gently rebuked her by informing her that she is not obligated to celebrate or recognize Veterans Day, Memorials Day, or Independence Day. And that the guaranteed rights under the Bill of Rights and the Civil rights should not automatically apply to her and her family as well.

The oddity of that dialogue came when the teacher expressed her concern about Our response. That teacher began calling us every "anti-" prefix in the English thesaurus to sum this up. In her subconscious mind, ad hominem tirades against our ancestors were enough in her classroom. Towards the end of that semester, the teacher later announced that she immigrated from Buenos Aires, Argentina.

The clairvoyant words of author, and conservative pundit Ann Coulter once said: "What ticks me off is you don't get to piggy-back off the black experience in America. So, okay; slavery, you got us. But you don't get to do that if you are a Woman, Immigrant, Gay, Hispanics. No. A lot of the Civil Rights, this is for the Black Americans. We seem to have forgotten them. It's not a rainbow coalition". Here, I agree with her comment up to the seventh dimension and beyond.

THE CENSUS: RACE & ETHNICITY IN THE UNITED STATES TODAY

Prior to the Nineteen Seventies everyone was deemed as white people, then black people, on government applications, military forms, bank loans, and contracts. It was John Rankins, Chairman of the Committee on World War who said, "The difficulties of the Negro are not the same as those of any other minority group for the simple reason that all the other monitories are considered as being white, and with but few isolated exceptions are treated as such". When the Great Society and New Deal was in full swing, the government began to break down the American population by Race & Ethnicity on its forms.

Every ten years, the American government conducts a census of everyone within its borders. The numbers are used for a myriad of different government programs, redistricting maps in the States, and for future programs and projects as deemed by Congress. I have enclosed a copy of the Census Questionnaire used in 2020 at the end of this chapter. I ask that you pay attention to blocks 5-7. This is how our government defines race & ethnicity today.

I perused through the 2010 and 2020 U.S. Census and was astonished to learn how our government categorizes its citizens. Although the 2020 census is not yet completed, I was still able to gather from it what I wanted. The federal government identifies race and ethnicity separately. Thus far, there are five racial groups. They are White or European, Black American with Caribbean & Africans, Asian American including American Indians and Pacific Islanders, People of two or more races or Bi-Racial Americans, and Hispanic and Latino Americans who are not identified as a race, but as an ethnicity, including Mexican, Cuban and Puerto Rican Americans. Those with other Spanish origins are counted as Others.

As of 2016 White Americans are the racial majority, making up Sixty-One percent of the entire population, including those Hispanic and Latino who categorize themselves as white. That increases the total white population to Seventy-Seven at percent.

The total population Hispanic & Latino Americans are Eighteen Percent, making them the largest minority group. They are not categorized as a racial group but as an ethnic group.

The total population of Black Americans is a little above Thirteen Percent. That number is inflated as you add Caribbean & African migrants to the count.

Asian Americans, Indians, and Pacific Islanders have the smallest number.

The 2016 census gives the regions of the country that all five groups ten to reside. For example, white Americans are the largest population in forty-eight states, with the exception of Alaska and Hawaii. But the highest white population compared to regions is the Midwest, with eighty-five percent. Forty-Two percent of Hispanic & Latino Americans live in the west with a growing population in South Florida, up the eastern corridors to the Northeast. Black Americans make up the largest population living in the south with Fifty-Five percent, with a growing population of Caribbean and African migrants populating South Florida, up to the Northeast. And with Forty-Eight percent of Asian & Pacific Islanders living in the west. It became perplexing to me seeing so many street signs written in different languages in our cities, and the number of different languages spoken when I am out and about. This was not the case when I was a child growing up in New Orleans. So here is what I found on my journey.

The current Administration is known as the "open borders administration". The sitting President today campaigned on an open border administration. Michelle Hackman of the "Wall Street Journal" wrote The Border Patrol made about 1.66 million arrests of migrants crossing the U.S-Mexico border illegally in the 2021 fiscal year. The number of unaccompanied children arriving at the border began to surge, leaving the administration scrambling to establish a network of makeshift shelters at convention centers and sports arenas, to ensure the children didn't languish in Border Patrol custody. This year (2021) nearly 145,000 children crossed the border without a parent. She went on to say "A confluence of events combined to bring about the record flow of migrants.

An economic collapse across Latin America pushed many people to move in search of work, just as the U.S. economy strengthened and as U.S. employers struggled to fill more than ten million job openings. Gang violence, autocratic crackdowns in several countries and extreme weather events, droughts in some regions, flooding in others pushed people to leave just as a new U.S. president took office with what was widely perceived as a welcoming tone." The article highlighted that not all of the migrants seeking entrance via the southern borders were from Latin American territories.

Caribbeans Migrants, Asian Migrants, Middle Eastern and African Migrants are also at a record scale. This article does not include legal migration but undocumented migration only. Liz Dee wrote of an earlier time in American history when a large scale of migration occurred and would have been categorized as open borders as well. Her article titled "The Mariel Boatlift", she writes "One of the most contentious events in mass migration started April 1, 1980, when several Cubans took control of a bus and drove it through a fence of the Peruvian embassy in Havana and were granted political asylum. Fidel Castro ultimately stated that the port of Mariel would be opened to anyone wishing to leave Cuba, as long as they had someone to pick them up. Cuban exiles in the U.S rushed to Key West in Miami to hire boats to transport people to the U.S. That set in motion a six-month drama in which more than one hundred twenty-five thousand Cubans fled their country and overwhelmed the shores of the U.S. The Cuban community in Florida launched every boat they owned or could charter at any price and headed to Cuba. The Cubans began arriving in Florida by the thousands. President Jimmy Carter welcomed them. Various domestic agencies began setting up refugee camps on military bases. By May over fifty-thousand refugees had already landed in the U.S. The American government provided Four Hundred Eighty Million Dollars to assist the newly arrived Cubans in settling in South Florida. The government also paid out compensation to the communities that were impacted by the Mariel boatlift event". Political pundits believe this was the event that was attributed to the incumbent Carter Administration, losing Forty-Six states in a landslide fashion in his 1980 re-election bid.

It took less than sixty years for this population to expand at the rate it has. It should be written here that Immigration is a marvelous tool for this country. It gets sour when the powers that be use biased measures to determine what population around the world is welcome and what population in the world is not. I can remember as far back questioning the friends I met from different backgrounds and languages. I even attempted to learn their language as best as I could. I enjoy eating their cuisine also.

So, when one U.S. Representative from the Fourteenth District of New York, (D), came to power, I anticipated hearing some stellar stories she would share of how she accomplished so much, so fast in her young political career. But then I figuratively witnessed her collapse behind the podium as she gave the keynote address at one of those civil rights programs. The rhetoric I continue to hear from her is how she is a woman of color (the identification my in laws were assigned on their birth certificates in the 1930's, where's her proof of that), she would lament that she is a descendant of slaves (both her parent are of Puerto Rican heritage so their toil would have been under the flag of Spain), she would oftentimes discuss her Jewish heritage, while other times she would insert Apartheid (a system of racial-genocide practiced in Southern Africa for centuries).

If this Representative was born on the island of Puerto Rico where her mother was born, she would be cast as a Mestizo or a Zambos. But since she resides within the shores of the mainland, she can self-identify herself as being a Zulu whenever it is plausible for her to do so.

She has a colleague in the U.S. House of Representatives. He represents the Third District of New York, (R). During his second run for the House, he filed his second personal financial disclosure report according to Date Santaliz and Liz Brown-Kaiser that he was "claiming his assets are as much as $11 million dollars.

That he obtained a degree from New York University.

That he addressed the Republican Jewish Coalition summit alleging he was of proud Jewish descent.

That his mother was in the twin towers of the World Trade Center in 9\11, and she survived the attack.

He was employed with Citigroup and with Goldman Sachs.

After the New York Times published its bombshell investigation, that Santos lied about his resume, the Congressman then began to admit that he did embellish his story.

His mother, who migrated to the U.S. from Brazil, who then married his Brazilian father; immigration record shows she was not in the United States on September 11, 2001.

New York University has no records of his enrollment.

That Citigroup and Goldman Sachs have no record of his employment.

The Congressman now says 'I never claimed to be Jewish. I am Catholic. Because I learned my maternal family had a Jewish background, I said I was Jew-ish'.

My concern is what happened to our intelligence and investigative offices? They are supposed to conduct thorough background checks on government employees of this caliber for Security Clearances. Also, I'm noticing a pattern forming. When you hear someone spewing what I call 'myth-storical', not historical events of their lives, recognize that they do so in order to legitimize their empty suit resume.

Freelance journalist Yvette Montoya posed this question in her article "Asian Latinx History Is Latin American History, So Why Are They Left Out?" She writes, "It's time to acknowledge that we Americans know very little about Latin American history. Even what we learn at the university level tends to center on Europe's invasion of the Americas. To understand Asian erasure in Latin America, look no further than the first contact Christopher Columbus had with the Taino people of Puerto Rico in 1492. He called them 'indios', which we know was a name meant for Indians from India; it's an erroneous term that persists to this day. Suppose Columbus legitimately believed he was in Asia. How is it that Asians have been so auspiciously left out of Latin American history when India was the intended destination of Columbus' journey? The Philippines was also in constant contact with both Spain and Nueva Espana (modern-day Mexico). Looking at the facts, it's pretty clear that the omission of Asians from Latin American history is deliberate and strategic. Dr Junyoung Veronica Kim, assistant professor of Latin American culture and literature at the University of Pittsburgh says we must go back further than the conquest of the Americas to understand why Asians have been omitted from history. The history of the orient is a long part of European identity. In the 15th century and the Middle Ages, Europe was not the power that it was in the 19th century. Columbus invaded the Caribbean during the height of the Ming Dynasty, which lasted from 1396-1644. Similarly, India's Mughal Empire was a global leader in 15th century trade and manufacturing. This all happened while Europe was still emerging from centuries of occupation, wars, famine, and disease.

Spain reconquered the Nasrid Kingdom of Granada ending some 800 year of Muslim Empire rule in the region. Spain and England had no real resources to trade, which helps us understand why they chose to colonize territories with resources violently. Enrique Dussel, a Mexican-Argentine philosopher wrote that the invention of the Americas that Europe's discovery narrative served as a covering up and a rewriting that puts Europe at the center of history, when in reality that was not the case. Recognizing Asia's economic superiority and Asians by proxy disrupts the identity of superiority that Europe was trying to create for itself. Latin America always thought of itself as an extension of Europe. This is plainly evident in the creation of the casta system in both Latin America and the Chino casta system in the Philippines since Spain colonized the Philippines and the Americas at the same time. Eventually a lot of these were grouped under indios that only people of African descent were to be slaves". Dr Kim says there is no quick fix when it comes to racism. I don't know how we can make it better. I think that's putting things idealistically. I think we can make a dent and try to make dents, but we need to start asking questions"? Bewildering and informative article here.

Asians in the U. S. have garnered a courageous reputation in the STEM sector of American society. Their dominance in those professions has the majority white ruling class kneeling. They are also a huge growing population mainly from China, Korea, and the Southeast area of the far east. I wondered for a long time how a "Chinatown" district in many large cities, promoting Asian own businesses only exists.

I found newspaper clippings of how foreign governments around the world are allowed to purchase real estate in the U.S., then employ dual citizens, with roots from the mainland as landlords and overseers of said property. So that is how it works.

Texas has introduced a law SB 147 that would ban citizens and government entities of China, Iran, North Korea and Russian from buying land in Texas, and it's already garnered support from many Republican legislators writes Han Li of the San Francisco Standard. She writes that "Nick Gee, a staff member of the civil rights organization Affirmative Action for Chinese calls the law a copy of anti-Asian land ownership laws, known as Alien Land Laws dating back to the late 19th and early 20th centuries that targeted Asian immigrants and restricted them from owning lands. People who are biased say it's just about foreigners versus citizens as if it is ok to be hostile to newcomers' '.

I observe that other underpinning issues are entangled with this story. A coworker of mine who attended an HBCU college in South Carolina told us stories of two different Chinese restaurants and one Asian own hamburger café parked directly across the street from campus. But when she and other classmates commuted to the predominantly white University of South Carolina campus there would be no Asian own business near the location. This reminds me of a chapter I wrote in my first book titled "The Forbidden Fruit or the Forbidden Truth in The Bible" (another must-read) where I discussed a particular line from Deuteronomy saying, "you shall be borrowers, and no one shall borrow from you".

Since the 1990's another spurt of immigrants began to arrive in the U.S. from the Continent of Africa. Odoh Chidubem of "Vocal Africa" explains why this increase occurred. He wrote "War and poverty is the stereotype the entire African continent has managed to earn for itself. As much as some people would hate, or even feel guilty to admit it, I'm from Africa evokes the image of someone who lives in a small village without internet and has to hunt for his food or a refugee fleeing from a war-torn country. Unfortunately, Africa has more than lived up to this stereotype. Armed conflict is still the continent's biggest challenge. According to OurWorldInData, a third of Sub-Saharan African countries were engaged in civil war in 1990. The Ethiopian Civil War was a conflict between the DERG government. Somalian warlords invaded the eastern part of the country then drought brought widespread deaths. Then there was the Rwandan genocide which took place. The major reason for the Rwandan war was class and not tribal reasons as many believe. The Germans in order to control the Rwandan populace, created a system that divided the people by class. They gave the Tutsi monarch military support, and the Tutsi social class administrative role. This led to a widened minor class divide that existed between the Hutus and the Tutsi tribes. At least Three Hundred Thousand Tutsis ran away to neighboring countries becoming refugees. Over one million people were killed, the one million people consisted of Tutsis, Twas and moderate Hutus. Odoh continued to describe other civil wars that broke out on the continent and that led to more refugees and asylum seeking.

The BBC Monitoring reported another civil war that erupted in the Sudanese capital, Khartoum as a direct result of a power struggle within the country's military leadership. It says, "The clashes are between the regular army and a paramilitary force called the Rapid Support Forces (RSF). It is disputed who fired the first shot but the fighting swiftly escalated in different parts of the country with more than four hundred civilians dying, according to the World Health Organization. The Sudanese air force mounted air strikes in the capital, a city of more than six million people, which is likely to have led to civilian casualties. The fighting is the latest episode in bouts of tension that followed the ousting of President Omar al-Bashir who came to power in a coup himself. Protests were calling for an end of the nearly three-decade rule and the army mounted a coup to get rid of him".

It was publisher Teddy Munene who voiced his dismay with the senseless outbreak of civil wars on the continent when he published the remarks of Russia's President Vladimir Putin. He writes "Russian President Vladimir Putin has once again given

Africans a reality check after he was quoted saying that the continent was like a graveyard for its people. When an African becomes rich, his bank accounts are in Switzerland. He travels to France for Medical treatment. He invests in Germany. He buys from Dubai. He consumes Chinese. He prays in Rome or Mecca. His children study in Europe. He travels to Canada, USA, for tourism. If he dies, he will be buried in his native country of Africa. Africa is just a cemetery for Africans. How can a cemetery be developed"?

Ironically, these are the migrants who denigrate Westerners calling us "AKATA'S", meaning wild dogs, when they immigrate to the West.

OMB No. 0607-1006: Approval Expires 11/30/2021

United States®
Census 2020

This is the official questionnaire for this address.
It is quick and easy to respond, and your answers are protected by law.

FOR
OFFICIAL
USE ONLY

Start here OR go online at my2020census.gov to complete your 2020 Census questionnaire.

Use a blue or black pen.

Before you answer Question 1, count the people living in this house, apartment, or mobile home using our guidelines.

- Count all people, including babies, who live and sleep here most of the time.
- If no one lives and sleeps at this address most of the time, go online at my2020census.gov or call the number on page 8.

The census must also include people without a permanent place to live, so:

- If someone who does not have a permanent place to live is staying here on April 1, 2020, count that person.

The Census Bureau also conducts counts in institutions and other places, so:

- Do not count anyone living away from here, either at college or in the Armed Forces.
- Do not count anyone in a nursing home, jail, prison, detention facility, etc., on April 1, 2020.
- Leave these people off your questionnaire, even if they will return to live here after they leave college, the nursing home, the military, jail, etc. Otherwise, they may be counted twice.

1. How many people were living or staying in this house, apartment, or mobile home on April 1, 2020?

Number of people =

2. Were there any additional people staying here on April 1, 2020 that you did not include in Question 1?

Mark X all that apply.

- ☐ Children, related or unrelated, such as newborn babies, grandchildren, or foster children
- ☐ Relatives, such as adult children, cousins, or in-laws
- ☐ Nonrelatives, such as roommates or live-in babysitters
- ☐ People staying here temporarily
- ☐ No additional people

3. Is this house, apartment, or mobile home — Mark X ONE box.

- ☐ Owned by you or someone in this household with a mortgage or loan? *Include home equity loans.*
- ☐ Owned by you or someone in this household free and clear (without a mortgage or loan)?
- ☐ Rented?
- ☐ Occupied without payment of rent?

4. What is your telephone number?

We will only contact you if needed for official Census Bureau business.

Telephone Number

FORM **DI-Q1** (10-31-2019)

11800018

Person 1

5. Please provide information for each person living here. If there is someone living here who pays the rent or owns this residence, start by listing him or her as Person 1. If the owner or the person who pays the rent does not live here, start by listing any adult living here as Person 1.

What is Person 1's name? *Print name below.*

First Name   MI

Last Name(s)

6. What is Person 1's sex? *Mark* X *ONE box.*

☐ Male ☐ Female

7. What is Person 1's age and what is Person 1's date of birth? *For babies less than 1 year old, do not write the age in months. Write 0 as the age.*

	Print numbers in boxes.		
Age on April 1, 2020	Month	Day	Year of birth

☐ years

→ **NOTE: Please answer BOTH Question 8 about Hispanic origin and Question 9 about race. For this census, Hispanic origins are not races.**

8. Is Person 1 of Hispanic, Latino, or Spanish origin?

☐ No, not of Hispanic, Latino, or Spanish origin

☐ Yes, Mexican, Mexican Am., Chicano

☐ Yes, Puerto Rican

☐ Yes, Cuban

☐ Yes, another Hispanic, Latino, or Spanish origin – *Print, for example, Salvadoran, Dominican, Colombian, Guatemalan, Spaniard, Ecuadorian, etc.*

9. What is Person 1's race?

Mark X *one or more boxes AND print origins.*

☐ White – *Print, for example, German, Irish, English, Italian, Lebanese, Egyptian, etc.*

☐ Black or African Am. – *Print, for example, African American, Jamaican, Haitian, Nigerian, Ethiopian, Somali, etc.*

☐ American Indian or Alaska Native – *Print name of enrolled or principal tribe(s), for example, Navajo Nation, Blackfeet Tribe, Mayan, Aztec, Native Village of Barrow Inupiat Traditional Government, Nome Eskimo Community, etc.*

☐ Chinese   ☐ Vietnamese   ☐ Native Hawaiian

☐ Filipino   ☐ Korean   ☐ Samoan

☐ Asian Indian   ☐ Japanese   ☐ Chamorro

☐ Other Asian – *Print, for example, Pakistani, Cambodian, Hmong, etc.*   ☐ Other Pacific Islander – *Print, for example, Tongan, Fijian, Marshallese, etc.*

☐ Some other race – *Print race or origin.*

→ **If more people were counted in Question 1 on the front page, continue with Person 2 on the next page.**

11800026

1. Print name of **Person 2**

First Name   MI

[   ] [   ]

Last Name(s)

[   ]

2. Does this person usually live or stay somewhere else?

Mark X all that apply.

☐ No

☐ Yes, for college   ☐ Yes, with a parent or
                                          other relative

☐ Yes, for a military assignment   ☐ Yes, at a seasonal or
                                          second residence

☐ Yes, for a job or business   ☐ Yes, in a jail or prison

☐ Yes, in a nursing home   ☐ Yes, for another reason

3. How is this person related to Person 1? *Mark X ONE box.*

☐ Opposite-sex husband/wife/spouse   ☐ Father or mother

☐ Opposite-sex unmarried partner   ☐ Grandchild

☐ Same-sex husband/wife/spouse   ☐ Parent-in-law

☐ Same-sex unmarried partner   ☐ Son-in-law or daughter-in-law

☐ Biological son or daughter   ☐ Other relative

☐ Adopted son or daughter   ☐ Roommate or housemate

☐ Stepson or stepdaughter   ☐ Foster child

☐ Brother or sister   ☐ Other nonrelative

4. What is this person's sex? *Mark X ONE box.*

☐ Male   ☐ Female

5. What is this person's age and what is this person's date of birth? *For babies less than 1 year old, do not write the age in months. Write 0 as the age.*

Print numbers in boxes.

Age on April 1, 2020   Month   Day   Year of birth

[   ]   [   ] [   ] [   ]
     /years

→ **NOTE: Please answer BOTH Question 6 about Hispanic origin and Question 7 about race. For this census, Hispanic origins are not races.**

6. Is this person of Hispanic, Latino, or Spanish origin?

☐ **No,** not of Hispanic, Latino, or Spanish origin

☐ Yes, Mexican, Mexican Am., Chicano

☐ Yes, Puerto Rican

☐ Yes, Cuban

☐ Yes, another Hispanic, Latino, or Spanish origin – *Print, for example, Salvadoran, Dominican, Colombian, Guatemalan, Spaniard, Ecuadorian, etc.* ⌐

[   ]

7. What is this person's race?

Mark X one or more boxes AND print origins.

☐ White – *Print, for example, German, Irish, English, Italian, Lebanese, Egyptian, etc.* ⌐

[   ]

☐ Black or African Am. – *Print, for example, African American, Jamaican, Haitian, Nigerian, Ethiopian, Somali, etc.* ⌐

[   ]

☐ American Indian or Alaska Native – *Print name of enrolled or principal tribe(s), for example, Navajo Nation, Blackfeet Tribe, Mayan, Aztec, Native Village of Barrow Inupiat Traditional Government, Nome Eskimo Community, etc.* ⌐

[   ]

☐ Chinese   ☐ Vietnamese   ☐ Native Hawaiian

☐ Filipino   ☐ Korean   ☐ Samoan

☐ Asian Indian   ☐ Japanese   ☐ Chamorro

☐ Other Asian – *Print, for example, Pakistani, Cambodian, Hmong, etc.* ⌐   ☐ Other Pacific Islander – *Print, for example, Tongan, Fijian, Marshallese, etc.* ⌐

☐ Some other race – *Print race or origin.* ⌐

[   ]

→ **If more people were counted in Question 1 on the front page, continue with Person 3 on the next page.**

3   11800034

1. Print name of **Person 3**

First Name   MI

Last Name(s)

2. Does this person usually live or stay somewhere else?

Mark X all that apply.

☐ No

☐ Yes, for college

☐ Yes, for a military assignment

☐ Yes, for a job or business

☐ Yes, in a nursing home

☐ Yes, with a parent or other relative

☐ Yes, at a seasonal or second residence

☐ Yes, in a jail or prison

☐ Yes, for another reason

3. How is this person related to Person 1? *Mark X ONE box.*

☐ Opposite-sex husband/wife/spouse

☐ Opposite-sex unmarried partner

☐ Same-sex husband/wife/spouse

☐ Same-sex unmarried partner

☐ Biological son or daughter

☐ Adopted son or daughter

☐ Stepson or stepdaughter

☐ Brother or sister

☐ Father or mother

☐ Grandchild

☐ Parent-in-law

☐ Son-in-law or daughter-in-law

☐ Other relative

☐ Roommate or housemate

☐ Foster child

☐ Other nonrelative

4. What is this person's sex? *Mark X ONE box.*

☐ Male   ☐ Female

5. What is this person's age and what is this person's date of birth? *For babies less than 1 year old, do not write the age in months. Write 0 as the age.*

Print numbers in boxes.

Age on April 1, 2020	Month	Day	Year of birth
years			

→ NOTE: Please answer BOTH Question 6 about Hispanic origin and Question 7 about race. For this census, Hispanic origins are not races.

6. Is this person of Hispanic, Latino, or Spanish origin?

☐ No, not of Hispanic, Latino, or Spanish origin

☐ Yes, Mexican, Mexican Am., Chicano

☐ Yes, Puerto Rican

☐ Yes, Cuban

☐ Yes, another Hispanic, Latino, or Spanish origin – *Print, for example, Salvadoran, Dominican, Colombian, Guatemalan, Spaniard, Ecuadorian, etc.* ⤹

7. What is this person's race?

Mark X one or more boxes AND print origins.

☐ White – *Print, for example, German, Irish, English, Italian, Lebanese, Egyptian, etc.* ⤹

☐ Black or African Am. – *Print, for example, African American, Jamaican, Haitian, Nigerian, Ethiopian, Somali, etc.* ⤹

☐ American Indian or Alaska Native – *Print name of enrolled or principal tribe(s), for example, Navajo Nation, Blackfeet Tribe, Mayan, Aztec, Native Village of Barrow Inupiat Traditional Government, Nome Eskimo Community, etc.* ⤹

☐ Chinese

☐ Filipino

☐ Asian Indian

☐ Vietnamese

☐ Korean

☐ Japanese

☐ Native Hawaiian

☐ Samoan

☐ Chamorro

☐ Other Asian – *Print, for example, Pakistani, Cambodian, Hmong, etc.* ⤹

☐ Other Pacific Islander – *Print, for example, Tongan, Fijian, Marshallese, etc.* ⤹

☐ Some other race – *Print race or origin.* ⤹

→ If more people were counted in Question 1 on the front page, continue with Person 4 on the next page.

1. Print name of **Person 4**

First Name   MI

Last Name(s)

2. Does this person usually live or stay somewhere else?

Mark ✗ all that apply.

- ☐ No

- ☐ Yes, for college
- ☐ Yes, for a military assignment
- ☐ Yes, for a job or business
- ☐ Yes, in a nursing home

- ☐ Yes, with a parent or other relative
- ☐ Yes, at a seasonal or second residence
- ☐ Yes, in a jail or prison
- ☐ Yes, for another reason

3. How is this person related to Person 1? *Mark ✗ ONE box.*

- ☐ Opposite-sex husband/wife/spouse
- ☐ Opposite-sex unmarried partner
- ☐ Same-sex husband/wife/spouse
- ☐ Same-sex unmarried partner
- ☐ Biological son or daughter
- ☐ Adopted son or daughter
- ☐ Stepson or stepdaughter
- ☐ Brother or sister

- ☐ Father or mother
- ☐ Grandchild
- ☐ Parent-in-law
- ☐ Son-in-law or daughter-in-law
- ☐ Other relative
- ☐ Roommate or housemate
- ☐ Foster child
- ☐ Other nonrelative

4. What is this person's sex? *Mark ✗ ONE box.*

- ☐ Male ☐ Female

5. What is this person's age and what is this person's date of birth? *For babies less than 1 year old, do not write the age in months. Write 0 as the age.*

Print numbers in boxes.

Age on April 1, 2020	Month	Day	Year of birth
years			

→ **NOTE: Please answer BOTH Question 6 about Hispanic origin and Question 7 about race. For this census, Hispanic origins are not races.**

6. Is this person of Hispanic, Latino, or Spanish origin?

- ☐ **No**, not of Hispanic, Latino, or Spanish origin
- ☐ Yes, Mexican, Mexican Am., Chicano
- ☐ Yes, Puerto Rican
- ☐ Yes, Cuban
- ☐ Yes, another Hispanic, Latino, or Spanish origin – *Print, for example, Salvadoran, Dominican, Colombian, Guatemalan, Spaniard, Ecuadorian, etc.*

7. What is this person's race?

Mark ✗ one or more boxes AND print origins.

- ☐ White – *Print, for example, German, Irish, English, Italian, Lebanese, Egyptian, etc.*

- ☐ Black or African Am. – *Print, for example, African American, Jamaican, Haitian, Nigerian, Ethiopian, Somali, etc.*

- ☐ American Indian or Alaska Native – *Print name of enrolled or principal tribe(s), for example, Navajo Nation, Blackfeet Tribe, Mayan, Aztec, Native Village of Barrow Inupiat Traditional Government, Nome Eskimo Community, etc.*

- ☐ Chinese
- ☐ Filipino
- ☐ Asian Indian
- ☐ Vietnamese
- ☐ Korean
- ☐ Japanese
- ☐ Native Hawaiian
- ☐ Samoan
- ☐ Chamorro

- ☐ Other Asian – *Print, for example, Pakistani, Cambodian, Hmong, etc.*
- ☐ Other Pacific Islander – *Print, for example, Tongan, Fijian, Marshallese, etc.*

- ☐ Some other race – *Print race or origin.*

→ **If more people were counted in Question 1 on the front page, continue with Person 5 on the next page.**

11800059

INFORMATIONAL COPY

1. Print name of **Person 5**

First Name   MI

Last Name(s)

2. Does this person usually live or stay somewhere else?

Mark X all that apply.

☐ No

☐ Yes, for college   ☐ Yes, with a parent or other relative

☐ Yes, for a military assignment   ☐ Yes, at a seasonal or second residence

☐ Yes, for a job or business   ☐ Yes, in a jail or prison

☐ Yes, in a nursing home   ☐ Yes, for another reason

3. How is this person related to Person 1? *Mark X ONE box.*

☐ Opposite-sex husband/wife/spouse   ☐ Father or mother

☐ Opposite-sex unmarried partner   ☐ Grandchild

☐ Same-sex husband/wife/spouse   ☐ Parent-in-law

☐ Same-sex unmarried partner   ☐ Son-in-law or daughter-in-law

☐ Biological son or daughter   ☐ Other relative

☐ Adopted son or daughter   ☐ Roommate or housemate

☐ Stepson or stepdaughter   ☐ Foster child

☐ Brother or sister   ☐ Other nonrelative

4. What is this person's sex? *Mark X ONE box.*

☐ Male   ☐ Female

5. What is this person's age and what is this person's date of birth? *For babies less than 1 year old, do not write the age in months. Write 0 as the age.*

Print numbers in boxes.

Age on April 1, 2020	Month	Day	Year of birth
_____ years			

→ NOTE: Please answer BOTH Question 6 about Hispanic origin and Question 7 about race. For this census, Hispanic origins are not races.

6. Is this person of Hispanic, Latino, or Spanish origin?

☐ **No,** not of Hispanic, Latino, or Spanish origin

☐ Yes, Mexican, Mexican Am., Chicano

☐ Yes, Puerto Rican

☐ Yes, Cuban

☐ Yes, another Hispanic, Latino, or Spanish origin – *Print, for example, Salvadoran, Dominican, Colombian, Guatemalan, Spaniard, Ecuadorian, etc.*

7. What is this person's race?

Mark X one or more boxes AND print origins.

☐ White – *Print, for example, German, Irish, English, Italian, Lebanese, Egyptian, etc.*

☐ Black or African Am. – *Print, for example, African American, Jamaican, Haitian, Nigerian, Ethiopian, Somali, etc.*

☐ American Indian or Alaska Native – *Print name of enrolled or principal tribe(s), for example, Navajo Nation, Blackfeet Tribe, Mayan, Aztec, Native Village of Barrow Inupiat Traditional Government, Nome Eskimo Community, etc.*

☐ Chinese   ☐ Vietnamese   ☐ Native Hawaiian

☐ Filipino   ☐ Korean   ☐ Samoan

☐ Asian Indian   ☐ Japanese   ☐ Chamorro

☐ Other Asian – *Print, for example, Pakistani, Cambodian, Hmong, etc.*

☐ Other Pacific Islander – *Print, for example, Tongan, Fijian, Marshallese, etc.*

☐ Some other race – *Print race or origin.*

→ If more people were counted in Question 1 on the front page, continue with Person 6 on the next page.

6   11800067

1. Print name of **Person 6**

First Name   MI

Last Name(s)

2. Does this person usually live or stay somewhere else?
Mark X all that apply.

- [ ] No

- [ ] Yes, for college
- [ ] Yes, for a military assignment
- [ ] Yes, for a job or business
- [ ] Yes, in a nursing home
- [ ] Yes, with a parent or other relative
- [ ] Yes, at a seasonal or second residence
- [ ] Yes, in a jail or prison
- [ ] Yes, for another reason

3. How is this person related to Person 1? *Mark X ONE box.*

- [ ] Opposite-sex husband/wife/spouse
- [ ] Opposite-sex unmarried partner
- [ ] Same-sex husband/wife/spouse
- [ ] Same-sex unmarried partner
- [ ] Biological son or daughter
- [ ] Adopted son or daughter
- [ ] Stepson or stepdaughter
- [ ] Brother or sister
- [ ] Father or mother
- [ ] Grandchild
- [ ] Parent-in-law
- [ ] Son-in-law or daughter-in-law
- [ ] Other relative
- [ ] Roommate or housemate
- [ ] Foster child
- [ ] Other nonrelative

4. What is this person's sex? *Mark X ONE box.*

- [ ] Male
- [ ] Female

5. What is this person's age and what is this person's date of birth? *For babies less than 1 year old, do not write the age in months. Write 0 as the age.*

Print numbers in boxes.

Age on April 1, 2020	Month	Day	Year of birth
years			

→ **NOTE: Please answer BOTH Question 6 about Hispanic origin and Question 7 about race. For this census, Hispanic origins are not races.**

6. Is this person of Hispanic, Latino, or Spanish origin?

- [ ] **No,** not of Hispanic, Latino, or Spanish origin
- [ ] Yes, Mexican, Mexican Am., Chicano
- [ ] Yes, Puerto Rican
- [ ] Yes, Cuban
- [ ] Yes, another Hispanic, Latino, or Spanish origin – *Print, for example, Salvadoran, Dominican, Colombian, Guatemalan, Spaniard, Ecuadorian, etc.*

7. What is this person's race?
Mark X one or more boxes AND print origins.

- [ ] White – *Print, for example, German, Irish, English, Italian, Lebanese, Egyptian, etc.*

- [ ] Black or African Am. – *Print, for example, African American, Jamaican, Haitian, Nigerian, Ethiopian, Somali, etc.*

- [ ] American Indian or Alaska Native – *Print name of enrolled or principal tribe(s), for example, Navajo Nation, Blackfeet Tribe, Mayan, Aztec, Native Village of Barrow Inupiat Traditional Government, Nome Eskimo Community, etc.*

- [ ] Chinese
- [ ] Filipino
- [ ] Asian Indian
- [ ] Other Asian – *Print, for example, Pakistani, Cambodian, Hmong, etc.*
- [ ] Vietnamese
- [ ] Korean
- [ ] Japanese
- [ ] Native Hawaiian
- [ ] Samoan
- [ ] Chamorro
- [ ] Other Pacific Islander – *Print, for example, Tongan, Fijian, Marshallese, etc.*

- [ ] Some other race – *Print race or origin.*

→ **If more people were counted in Question 1 on the front page, continue with Person 7 on the next page.**

> Use this section to complete information for the rest of the people you counted in Question 1 on the front page.
> *We may call for additional information about them.*

Person 7

First Name

MI

Last Name(s)

Sex
☐ Male ☐ Female

Age on April 1, 2020
_____ years

Date of Birth
Month Day Year of birth

Related to Person 1?
☐ Yes ☐ No

Person 8

First Name

MI

Last Name(s)

Sex
☐ Male ☐ Female

Age on April 1, 2020
_____ years

Date of Birth
Month Day Year of birth

Related to Person 1?
☐ Yes ☐ No

Person 9

First Name

MI

Last Name(s)

Sex
☐ Male ☐ Female

Age on April 1, 2020
_____ years

Date of Birth
Month Day Year of birth

Related to Person 1?
☐ Yes ☐ No

Person 10

First Name

MI

Last Name(s)

Sex
☐ Male ☐ Female

Age on April 1, 2020
_____ years

Date of Birth
Month Day Year of birth

Related to Person 1?
☐ Yes ☐ No

Thank you for completing your 2020 Census questionnaire.

FOR OFFICIAL USE ONLY

JIC1 JIC2

If your enclosed postage-paid envelope is missing, please mail your completed questionnaire to:

U.S. Census Bureau
[Address Removed]

If you need help completing this questionnaire, call toll-free 1-844-330-2020, Sunday through Saturday from 7:00 a.m. to 2:00 a.m. ET.

TDD — Telephone display device for the hearing impaired. Call toll-free 1-844-467-2020, Sunday through Saturday from 7:00 a.m. to 2:00 a.m. ET.

The U.S. Census Bureau estimates that completing the questionnaire will take 10 minutes on average. Send comments regarding this burden estimate or any other aspect of this burden to: Paperwork Reduction Project 0607-1006, U.S. Census Bureau, DCMD-2H174, 4600 Silver Hill Road, Washington, DC 20233. You may email comments to <2020.census.paperwork@census.gov>. Use "Paperwork Reduction Project 0607-1006" as the subject.

This collection of information has been approved by the Office of Management and Budget (OMB). The eight-digit OMB approval number 0607-1006 confirms this approval. If this number were not displayed, we could not conduct the census.

11800083

EMANCIPATION COMPENSATION PROPOSAL

During the civil battle between the States, President Lincoln was in favor of indemnifying slave Owners in the south for the emancipation of their Negro slaves.

According to renowned Historian John H Franklin, he went so far as to write a draft of the bill, which provided for gradual emancipation and another which provided that the federal government would share the expenses of compensating masters for their slaves." After all, the original ratified draft of the U.S. Constitution was a pre slavery ratification as in Article I, Section Three, where it says "Taxes shall be apportioned among the several states which may be included within this union, according to their respective numbers, which shall be determined by adding the whole number of free-person, including those bound to Service for a term of years (indentured servants), and excluding Indians not taxed, three fifth of all others". The three-fifths of all other were the Negros slave population in the South. They were not bound for a term of a year as the indentures were. They were bound to be slaves in perpetuity.

Article 1, Section (9), (1) says, "the migration of Importation of Such Persons as any of the States now existing shall think proper to admit, shall not be prohibited by the Congress prior to the Year One Thousand Eight Hundred and Eight, but a tax or duty may be imposed on such Importation not exceeding ten dollars for each person (slave)". This clause prohibited the congress from interfering with the importation of slaves arriving in the south, before 1808 as sanctioned by the Federal Government. But it also allowed the federal government to tax the border states a fee of ten dollars for each slave imported. So, the federal government profited with compensatory taxes from the human horror as did the southern states. Meaning Northern states were allocated compensation also.

The border states or the southern states openly, pro-slavery territories. They even drafted pro-slavery clauses in their state constitutions. For example, my home state of Louisiana drafted pro-slavery Article's such as Article 35. A slave is in the power of a master to whom he belongs. The master may sell him, dispose (murder) of his person, his industry, and his labor.' he can do nothing, possess nothing, or acquire anything, but what must belong to his master. Article 174. The slave is incapable of making any kind of contract, except those which relate to his own emancipation.

Article 175. All that a slave possesses belongs to his master; he possesses nothing of his own, except his peculium (personal property as might be held by a slave), that is to say, the sum of money or movable estate which his master chooses he should possess. Article 177. The slave is incapable of exercising any public office or private trust, he cannot be tutor, curator, executor, nor attorney, he cannot be a witness in either civil or criminal matters. He cannot be a party in any civil action, either as plaintiff or defendant. Article 181. The master may discharge himself from such responsibility by abandoning his slave to the person injured; in which case, such person shall sell such slave at public auction, in the usual form, to obtain payment of the dames and costs, and the balance, if any, shall be returned to the master. I will run out of electricity in my home before I run out of pro-slavery legislation. Highlighting the enforcement side of said legislation would properly equal the same amount of electricity.

As part of President Lincoln's redress, the enslaver would receive four hundred dollars for each slave in his custody; plus, less than one half days cost of the war. For example, the State of Virginia was determined to have slaves at the time of the proposal. So, the total number of federal bonds to be paid to that state alone would have been $196,354,800 in restitution to slave owners for the emancipation of their slaves, if passed by both Chambers.

Another proposal to the same bill read, "every state, wherein slavery now exists, which shall abolish the same therein, at any time, or times, before the first day of January, in the year of our Lord One Thousand and Nine Hundred (1900), shall receive compensation from the United States". This proposal meant that every southern state had up to, but no later than thirty-seven years to emancipate their negro slaves in order for them to receive any compensation.

Lastly, President Lincoln used the census of 1860 to determine the number of slaves in each pro-slavery state. Historian Allen Guelzo wrote that "twenty out of the twenty-eight border representatives and senators politely declined to act on his plea". In their letter of disapproval to the President, the Majority wrote "The undersigned, Representatives of Kentucky, Virginia, Missouri, Tennessee, Delaware, and Maryland in the two houses of congress. We have given it a most respectful consideration, and now lay before you, our response. A few of our members voted for the resolution recommended by your message of the Sixth of March last, the greater portion of us did not and we will briefly state the prominent reasons that influenced our action: Many of us doubted the constitutional power of this government to make appropriations of money for the object designated, through our finances were in ono condition to bear the immense outlay which it's adoption and execution would impose upon the national treasury.

According to the Census of 1860, there were then very nearly four million slaves in the country; they exceed that number now. We did not feel that we should be justified in voting for a measure that, if carried out, would add this vast amount to our public debt, at a moment when the treasury was reeling under the enormous expenditure of the war. The right to hold slaves is a right appertaining to all States of this Union. They have the right to cherish or abolish the institution as their tastes or their interest may prompt, and no one is authorized to question the right, or limit its enjoyment, it is a war against nationality to maintain and preserve its rights of property and domestic safety which is made to be assailed by this government. Can it mean, that by abandoning Slavery in our States, we are removing pressure from you and the country, conceding to each state and its loyal citizens their just rights, and we are married to you by indissoluble ties. Do tis, Mr. President, and you touch the American heart and invigorate it with new hopes, and you will in due time, restore peace to your country, life despair to a future of glory, and preserve to your countryman, their prosperity, and to man the inestimable treasure of constitutional government. We cannot trust anything to the contingencies of future legislation. If congress, shall provide sufficient funds and place them at your disposal, to be applied by

106

you, to the payment of any of our States or the citizens thereof, who shall adopt the abolishment of slavery, either gradual or immediate as they may determine, then will our States and people take this proposition into careful consideration".

It was Biographer Ida Tarbell, who wrote the following, "Although the message failed to arouse the border states, one-million dollars was appropriated by Congress to pay slaveholders in the District of Columbia for the immediate emancipation of their slaves". Not one red copper penny has ever been appropriated too this day, to monetarily compensate the negro-slaves, nor their direct descendants, for the planetary force trauma brought down on them inside these borders.

Let us look at some modern-day reparations that have been allocated then and now. Our government uses the revenue it collects via taxes, bonds, and investments to name a few. After the Constitutional duties are met, our elected officials will use the revenue as they see fit. For example, you may say I do not want Three Billion Eight Hundred Million dollars of my taxes to go to a government in the middle east whose Knesset drafts legislation to criminalize Christian Evangelicals with jail time, if they teach the Gospels of Christ in Jerusalem. Someone else may say, I do not want One Billion Six Hundred Million dollars of my taxes to go to a Pro Choice Organization via the Paycheck Protection Program. However, due to political action coalitions, your concerns will remain just that.

Due to Treaties signed with Native Tribes during the colonial period, tribal members are entitled to receive per capita benefits in accordance with the Tribal Revenue Allocation Plan approved by the Department of Interior. A neighbor of mine years ago, was a member of the Porch Creek Indians. She shared with me a letter of her eligibility for benefits. I posted a redacted copy of that letter for your curiosity. She has two young boys who are eligible for benefits as well.

POARCH BAND OF CREEK INDIANS

5811 Jack Springs Road • Atmore, Alabama 36502
Tribal Offices: (251) ███████
www.poarchcreekindians ███████

July 31, 2017

RE: Per Capita for year 2016

To Whom It May Concern:

████████ is a Tribal Member of the Poarch Band of Creek Indians. As such, she is entitled to receive the following per capita benefit:

Per capita: Per capita distributions are in accordance with our Tribal Revenue Allocation Plan which is approved by the Department of the Interior. Per capita distributions may vary annually depending on our Tribal Revenues and does not constitute earned income.

The total distribution for 2016 was $24,315.56, all of which was less 10% tax withholdings. This distribution was received in January of 2016.

For further information, please contact our office.

Thank you,

Tabatha Davis

Tribal Member Benefits
251-████, Extension ████

Seeking Prosperity and Self Determination

After the attack on the fleet in Pearl Harbor Hawaii, survey showed that the majority of Americans feared that persons of Japanese ancestry on the west coast would act as spies and created a security risk. President Theodore Roosevelt enacted Executive Order 9012 in 1942 that established the War Relocation Act that administered internment camps (that lasted from 1942-1946) for over one hundred twenty thousand Japanese families. According to the San Francisco Chronicle, the first directive to remove Japanese families was sent by the Western Defense Command and Fourth Army Wartime Civil Control Administration, commanded by Lieutenant General John L Dewitt. The directive read "All Japanese persons, both aliens and non-aliens, will be evacuated from the above-designated area by 12 o'clock noon in April 1942. No Japanese person will be permitted to enter or leave the above-described area without obtaining special permission from the Provost Marshall". They were told that their homes, businesses and many other assets they owned would be in place whenever the war ended. But many of them sold their properties and business at a fracture of the market value.

The interns were fed meals described as mass-produced army-style grubs. In an effort to redress the wrongs brought down on the families, President Harry S Truman signed the Japanese Evacuation Claims Act of 1948 that allocated Thirty-Eight Million dollars in compensation. In 1988 President Ronald Reagan signed into law the Civil Liberties Act that allocated Twenty Thousand dollar payments to every internee, evacuee, of Japanese ancestry who suffered due to the discriminatory action by the Federal Government during World War II. Soon after, a civil lawsuit was filed in 1996 by five Japanese Latin Americans who were deported from their homes in Latin America during the war and were forced into internment camps in the United States. They were awarded Five Thousand dollars for each family member of Japanese Latin American Ancestry and given an Apology from the office of the President as undocumented aliens. It is estimated that One Billion Six Hundred Million dollars in compensations were paid under these two Acts. During the internment, the internees had no impediments in place to rob them of any future wealth they inherited. Their families remained intact. They were not broken or separated. They were fortunate enough to escape obstructive public laws like Article 182-Slaves cannot marry without the consent of their masters, and their marriages do not produce any of the civil effects which result from such contract. Article 183-Children born of a mother then in a state of slavery, whether married or not, follow the condition of their mother, they are consequently slaves, and belong to the master of their mother. Article 631-He who has the use of one or more slaves or animals has the right to enjoy their service for his wants and those of his family.

Dignity, pride, and a sense of patriotism were restored to the families and descendants who were victims of those internment camps.

Holocaust Survivors: "The Obama administration awarded $12 million to Holocaust survivors. The allocation from the Department of Health and Human Services to the Jewish Federations of North America, to disburse over five years, is part of an initiative launched by Vice president Joe Biden in 2013 It addresses the needs of survivors in the United States a quarter of whom live below the poverty line. Combined with matching private funds, the approximately $2.5 million per year over the five years will support $4.1 million in programming annually for organizations that help Holocaust survivors. Mark Wilf, Chairman said These are our mothers and our fathers, our teachers and our mentors. They deserve to live their remaining years in dignity, and this award will help make that hope a reality". Now the Obama administration stood ten toes down in pronouncing any monetary forms of redress to the direct descendents of slaves in the United States. But he allocated targeted funds to these Survivors.

The "Little Shell Tribe: A Federal Recognition Bill Goes to the President" is the title of an article written by Jonathon Ambarian. It reads "The Little Shell tribe of Chippewa Indians of Montana has fought a decades long battle to win federal recognition. Now, that effort is on its way to President Donald Trump's desk. The U.S Senate gave final approval to the National Defense Authorization Act, a major defense funding bill that included Little Shell recognition as an amendment. The U.S. House passed the bill a week earlier. Senator Jon Tester said If you're Little Shell, you know

110

how big of a day this is. It might not seem like a big deal to the folks who aren't impacted, but the truth is that this is going to allow the Little Shell to really move forward in a sway that they've been trying to do for 150 years. The bill has in addition to allowing the Little Shell access to federal funding, and services, the legislation also states the U.S. The Department of Interior shall acquire 200 acres to serve as a land base for the tribe headquartered in Great Falls Montana ''. Even as modern as 2019 reparations bills have been introduced by competent law makers, and passed in both Chambers, then signed by Presidents. There were no exploratory committees convened. No public meetings to voice opposition to the bill. Instead, just a desire to get it done by the Legislative and Executive branches of government.

Reuters published an astonishing report titled "Explore the U.S. Elite's Ties to Slavery". It is a list of the current Presidents, Senators, Representatives, and Governors whose family were slave owners. Their list includes President's Jimmy Carter, Bill Clinton, George H. Bush, Barack Obama's mothers side of the family, and current President Joseph Biden. It is a must read highlighting the success that generational wealth passed down to your descendents can accomplish.

In a recent landmark U.S. Supreme Court decision Justice Clarence Thomas referenced in his opinion the: The Freemen's Bureau Bill '' that was created after the civil war in 1865 by President Lincoln and by an act of Congress to aid the newly freed slaves with education, health care, employment contracts with private landowners and land. Sort of a modern day Marshall Plan. This was a U.S. sponsored program designed to rehabilitate the economies of western and southern European countries after the world wars, in order to create stable conditions in which they could survive. The Freemens Bill was designed to redress the harms carried out by this government against a specific group of people, knowingly, the newly legalized negroe people. All the benefactors of that Bill were the colonists as the term Refugee's was later added to it. Also due to the lack of oversight and enforcement, the Bill ended with one year of its passages. And the targeted group was left empty-handed, probably by design.

The Freemaens Bill was not initially an all-lives-matter Bill because not all races of people alive at that time were negatively disenfranchised by two centuries of legalized chattel bondage...ie the Native Indians, the European immigrants, and other newcomers. The negro paupers were the targeted demographics because they carried the fresh scars of generational oppression. So today, legislation similar to the Freemens Bill must be allocated to their descendents for the due's the Freemen paid. It should not be based upon race, that includes any of these made-up demographics called minorities, or people of color today. These are largely the children of documented and undocumented immigrants. Whatever grievances they find against the United States Government, they have to be filed under separate cover away from any actions the direct descendents of the Freemen may have. The auspicious success of the Million Man March held on the Mall of Washington D.C. where more than two million participants participated featured numerous speakers addressing these sentiments.

I would like to share a famous speech given by a once in a generation orator: "Five score years ago, a great American, in whose symbolic shadow we stand today, signed the Emancipation Proclamation. This momentous decree came as a great beacon light of hope to millions of Negro slaves who had been seared in the flames of withering injustice. it cae as a joyous daybreak to end the lon night of their captivity. But 100 years later, the Negro still is not free. One hundred years later, the life of the Negro is till sadly crippled by the mancies of segregation and the chanins of discrimination. One hundred years later, the Negro lives on on a lonely island of poverty in the midst of a vast ocean of material prosperity. The Negro is still languished in the corners of American society and finds himself in exile in his own land. And so we've come here today to dramatize a shameful condition. In a sense we've come to our nation's capital to cash a check.

When the architects of our republic wrote the magnificent words of the Constitution and the Declaration of Independence, they signed a promissory note to which every American was to fall heir. This note was a promise that all men- Black and white men- would be guaranteed the unalienable rights of life, liberty and the pursuit of happiness. It is obvious today that America has defaulted on this promissory note insofar as her citizens of color are concerned. Insted of honoring this sacred obligation, Americas has given the Negro people a bad check, a check which has come back marked as insufficient funds. But we refuse to believe that the bank of justice is bankrupt.We refuse to believe that there are insufficient funds in this nation's great vaults of opportunity. And se we've come to cash this check, a check that will give us upon demand the riches of freedom and the security of justice. It would be fatal for the nation to overlook the moment's urgency. This sweltering summer of the Negro legitimate discontent will not pass until there is an invigorating autumn of freedom and equality. We must forever conduct our struggle on the high plane of dignity and discipline. We must not allow our creative protest to degenerate into physical violence.We can never be satisfied as long as the Negro is the victim of the unspeakable horrors of police brutality. We cannot be satisfied as long as the negro basic mobility is from a smaller ghetto to a larger one.So even though we face the difficulties of today and tomorrow, I still have a dream. It is a dream deeply rooted in the American dream"

This excerpt came from the "I Have a Dream " speech delivered on August 28, 1963 on the steps of the Lincoln Memorial (which Is the photo selected as the cover of my book), by the Reverend, Doctor Martin L. King.

These words were delivered one year prior to my birth. In his speech he used the phrase "Black boys and Black girls, Color people, and Negro. In fact, i counted the Negro beings used fourteen times in his original speech. These terms are important because they describe the demographics he represented. The word Negro is on my birth certificate. I have relatives who have Colored on their birth record. So it is abundantly clear who the Reverend amplified during his oration. It is also abundantly clear those he did not include in his oration. So when you hear those whom we call the culture-colonizers of today misrepresent his lecture for their own preconceived proclivities, you can refer to the true demographics the Reverend was representing. And those he was not.

Concluding, I want to express my gratitude to the precedent setting Task-Force in the Golden State of California for their monumental victory for the cause...

Here you have it. A readers-digest manuscript from A Foundational Born, U.S. American. The land I was born in...The land I was educated in...The land I own property in...The land I pay taxes in... The military I volunteered to serve in...The land I retired in. And the land I will expire in.

ABOUT THE AUTHOR

The Author is a Foundation Born, U.S. American. Meaning his parents did not immigrate. His lineage can be traced back to the first segregated Census taken in 1860, and beyond. He was born in the Big Easy, where both his parents emigrated too from neighboring Mississippi. Mr. Rowan is a graduate of Loyola University in New Orleans, and he completed the Federal Law Enforcement Training Academy (FLET-X) in Glynco, Georgia, he is a veteran of the United States Navy, where he was attached to the aircraft carrier USS AMERICA (CV-66) and was awarded Three Ribbons and Two Medals during his brief tour. He retired from twenty-five years of public service and is the owner of a small LLC in the panhandle area of Northwest Florida. You can also purchase his Books and eBooks from Amazon Kindle Books. Or you may purchase them from his website at "Teambfm.net " where you can find other merchandise, as well as read his blogs. If you enjoy his content, then consider clicking on the donate button at the top right corner on his site and do so. His PayPal account is teambfm22.

BIBLIOGRAPHIES

Allosso, Dan, "Cotton Is King", U.S. History and Primary Source Anthology, Volume I.

Ambarian, Jonathon, "Little Shell Tribe federal recognition bill goes to President", MTN News, December 2019.

Anderson, Trezzvant, W., "Come Out Fighting", Long Island, NY; 761 Tank Battalion and Allied Veterans Association, 1979 page 21, reprinted from 1945.

Athey, Amber, "You Built This Nation", Daily Caller, March 6, 2019.

Barton, David, "American History in Black & White", copyrights First Edition, 2004, pages 103-108.

Bennett, Michael, "When Dreams Come True: The GI Bill", by Brassey's, copyright 1996.

Bergam, Peter, M., "The Chronological History of the Negro in America, New York: New York American Library, 1969, page 604.

Brown, Williams, W., "The Black Man, His Antecedents and his Achievements", page 179."

Buckley, Gail, "American Patriots", Random House, 2001.

Cash, W.J., "The Mind of the South", New York, Doubleday, 1956, page 78.

Cashin, Herschel, V., "Under Fire with the Tenth Cavalry", New York: Bellwether Publishing, 1970.

Chidubem, Odoh, "8 Civil Wars In Africa", Vocal Africa, November 2019.

Coffman, Edward, M., "The Old Army", New York: Oxford University Press, 1986.

Connell, Evan, S., "Son of the Morning Star".

Coulter, Ann, "Adios, American", Regnery Publishing, page 248.

Dee, Liz, "A Flood of Cuban Migrants-The Mariel Boatlift", Association for Diplomatic Studies & Training, April 2015.

Delvingene, Lawrence, Januta, Andrea, Koh, Gui Oning, Heath, Brad, Lasseter, Tom, Explore The U.S. Elite's Ties to Slavery". Reuters Jun e 2023.

Dennison, Sam, "Scandalize My Name", New York: Garland, 1982, page 243.

Drew, Charles, "The Journal of Southern History", Volume XII, Number 3, August 1975, Copyright 1975 by the Southern Historical Association

Drinnon, Richard, "Facing West", New York", New York: New American Library, 1990.

Drontning, Phillip, "Black Heroes in Our Nation's History", page 103.

Executive Order 9981: Desegregation of the Armed Forces (1948), National Archives, July 1948.

Franklin, John, H. and Moss, Alfred A., "From Slavery to Freedom", Published by Alfred A Knopf, Inc.

Farewell, Byron, "Over There", New York: W. W. Norton & Company, 1999, page 149.

Fikes, Robert, "Milton S.J. Wright (1903-1972), Black Past: contributor, September 14, 2020.

Frasier, Gerald, C., "Book Recalls Black World War II Tank Battalion", The New York Times, September 5, 1983.

Frydle, Kathleen, J., "The GI Bill", Cambridge University Press, copyrights.

Giatti, Ian M., Israeli bill criminalizing evangelism". Christian Post Reporter. March 25023.

Godwin, Doris, K., "No Ordinary Time", page 329.

Guelzo, Allen, Cl, "Lincoln's Emancipation Proclamation, The End of Slavery in America".

Hackman, Michelle, "Border Patrol Makes 1.66 million Arrest", Wall Street Journal, October 2021.

Horowitz, Helen, L., "Campus Life", University of Chicago Press.

Jordan, Winthrop, D., "White Over Black: American Attitudes Toward the Negro, 1550-1812", Copyright 1968 by the University of North Carolina Press.

Klarman, Michael, J., "The White Primary ruling", Florida State University Law Review, volume 29, 2001.

Keegan, John, "The First World War", New York: Knopf, 1999, page 52

Leonard R Harmon, "African American Registry", published January 21, 1917.

Li, Han, "Texas Bill Barring Chinese Real Estate Ownership Renes Anti-Asian Racism Debate", San Francisco Standard, February 2023.

Lieberman, Robert, C., "Shifting the Color Line: Race and the American Welfare State", Harvard University Press, 2001.

Long, E.B., "The Civil War Day by Day", Garden City, NJ, 1971, pages 700-725.

Maeder, Jay, "Fighting Heart, Flip Corkin 1943", New York Daily News, June 15, 1998.

McPherson, James, M. "The Negro's Civil War", page 169.

Morgan, Jean, S. New York Times: Random House, 1991, page 61.

Montoya, Yvette, "Asian Latinx History Is Latin American History, So Why Are They Left Out?", Freelance Bakersfield Los Angeles, July 2022.

Munene, Teddy, "Africa Is A Cemetery For Africans", Politics, November 2018.

Murray, Pauli, "State Laws on Race and Color", New York: Women's Division of Christian Services, 1950.

Myrdal, Gunnar, "An American Dilemma", Routledge, Volume I, 1944.

Nell, William, C., "Colored Patriots of the American Revolution", Salem, N.H: Ayers, 1986, reprinted from 1855 preface.

Ochieng, Beverly, "Sudan: Why has fighting broken out there"?, BBC Monitoring, Nairobi, April 2023.

Rowan, Carl, T., "Breaking Barriers", Boston: Little, Brown & Company, 1981.

Santaliz, Kate, and Brown-Kaiser, Liz, "A timeline of Rep. George Santos fabrications and controversy", NBC News Capitol Hill Team, September 2023.

Sarah H Bradford: "Scenes in the Life of Harriet Tubman": Logan and Winston, Dictionary of American Negro Biography, page 544.

Scott, Emmet, J., "Official History of the American Negro in the World War", pages 276-277.

Lewis-Stempel, John, "Germany's Colonial Genocide in Namibia", Daily Express, January 2014.

Sterner, Richard, "Negro Share: A Study of Income, Consumption, Housing, and Public Assistance", Published November 7, 2008.

Suggs, Ernie, "Emory Apologizes to Medical School Applicant", Atlanta-Journal Constitution, June 2021.

Tarbell, Ida, "Ida Tarbell & Abraham Lincoln: A History at Home".

Thomas, Williams, G., "The Growth of Slavery and Southern Railroad Development", University of Nebraska, Lincoln, 2006-2017.

Thompson, Reuben, H., "Letters of Reuben Thompson", National Farm Labor Union, May 7, 1946 Page 523.

Turner, Sarah, E., and Bound, John, "Closing the Gap or Widening the Divide", National Bureau of Economic Research, 2002.

Washington, Jewish Telegraphic Agency, "Obama administration earmarks $12M for Holocaust Survivors October 2015.

Wilkins, Roy, "The Crisis", Publisher, NAACP Magazine, 1949-1950.

Weitz, Sonia, S., "My Black Messiah came for me".

Wright, Steven, "The Civil Liberties Act of 1988", Dartmouth History & Education.